£14.95

The Image Factory

D1634709

THE LIBRARY
SAINT FRANCIS XAVIER
SIXTH FORM COLLEGE
MALWOOD ROAD, SW12 8EN

The Image Factory

Fads and Fashions in Japan

Donald Richie

with photos by Roy Garner

REAKTION BOOKS

SAINT FRANCIS XAVIER
SIXTH FORM COLLEGE
MALWOOD ROAD SW12 8EN

1|7|03 LIBRARY 14.95

306
28668
306 0952 RIC

Published by Reaktion Books Ltd
79 Farringdon Road
London ECIM 3JU

First published 2003

Copyright © Reaktion Books 2003

Donald Richie is hereby identified as the author of
this work in accordance with section 77 of the
Copyright, Designs and Patents Act of 1998.

Roy Garner is identified as the photographer of the pictures in this book.

All rights reserved.

No part of this publication may be reproduced, stored in a retrieval system,
or transmitted, in any form or by any means, electronic, mechanical,
photocopying, recording or otherwise, without the prior permission
of the publishers.

Printed and bound in Hong Kong

British Library Cataloguing in Publishing Data
Richie, Donald, 1924–
      The image factory: fads and fashions in Japan
      1. Fads – Japan 2. Japan – Social life and customs – 1945 –
      1. Title II. Garner, Roy
      306' .0952

ISBN 1 86189 153 9

Contents

The age demanded an image
Of its accelerated grimace . . .

Ezra Pound

Foreword

Imēji cheinji – a phrase ('image change') often on the lips of young Japanese upon their denoting some difference in the appearance of their friends: hair dyed a novel shade, something odd in the way of sunglasses, a new cell-phone with e-mail adaptability and a Tweetie-Bird strap instead of a Hello-Kitty. Though sometimes used in an ironic sense (as when the friend has, for example, put on a discernible amount of weight) the term usually indicates pleasure and approval.

This is because, in a place so status conscious as Japan, self-image is important and new image indicators are in demand. All indicate, to be sure, merely how to be different in a manner everyone else will shortly be. Nevertheless, or consequently, a demand for the new indicator grows and an industry accommodates mass production. This is everywhere true, but Japanese society includes conformism as a major ingredient and everyone wanting to do everything at the same time creates a need which the fad and fashion factories fill.

Fashion (not just in clothing, but in gadgets, attitudes, beliefs) is the major means through which image is changed and, since its rate of mutation is so extreme, the factories must turn out novelty in mass – at which point it ceases to be novelty. The successful and self-perpetuating factory which is Japan's image enterprise has operated for centuries but it is only now, in this age of instant communication, that it reveals itself as a major industry.

As William Gibson, scholar of the Japanese new, has noted, 'cultural change is essentially technologically driven . . . the Japanese have been doing it for more than a century now and they really do have a head start on the rest of us.'

Just as an individual contrives a style, a collection of images the purpose of which is integration and the effect of which is presentation, so a nation collectively projects an appearance, a 'national style'. This is made of various layers. The bottom finds the immutables, those assumptions often fictionalized as 'national character'. Up nearer the surface floats fashion, changeable but sometimes more abiding. And frothing on the surface frolics fad.

All are devoted to serving the particular interests of a controlling culture, of promoting an agenda-filled consensus on how the human condition is to be usefully encountered. Yet each is individual in that it has a role to play.

In its columns devoted to a definition of the term *Webster's Unabridged* says that style is (among other things) 'a distinctive or characteristic mode of presentation, construction, or execution in any art, employment, or product'. It is thus a manner of indicating, identifying something which might not otherwise be visible. As Lord Chesterfield said: 'Style is the dress of thought.'

A fad, on the other hand, is 'a custom, amusement or the like, followed for a time with exaggerated zeal'. Its nature is in its popularity and gives society at large a way through which all can be interested in the same things at the same time, an activity which lends the impression of solidarity. All cultures are susceptible and sometimes fads even turn into more permanent fashions.

By definition a fad is novel. It always appears from outside, either spatially or temporarily. That it comes from elsewhere is indeed one of its attractions. Another is its consequent degree of freshness. Most fads do not have long shelf-lives and must perhaps, therefore, if they are to sell, have the air of the very recent.

In Japan – like Britain an assortment of small islands – that which is outside much more defines the inside than in, say, large land masses such as Russia or North America. Fads constantly crash against these island coasts and sweep across the archipelagos with hurricane force. In Japan these are as welcome as the harvest-making rain, for if the country did not have fads from abroad to import and adapt it would not be able to define itself.

This is true, of course, of all countries. Honest English victuals are to be defined through imported Mediterranean food. French quality cooking is defined against imported American fast-food junk. In Japan, however, the process is not only much exaggerated but also made much more visible. And, as in all countries, the determining new fashion comes, almost by definition, from elsewhere.

There are reasons for this. As Gregory Clark has said:

To explain Japan, we need go no further than the fact that it was an isolated society that . . . was able to borrow from and absorb other civilizations without being occupied, colonized, or seriously threatened. It was therefore able to retain its original isolationist island values while creating the modern industrialized society we see today. It is the tribe that became a nation.

Since the middle of the nineteenth century, foreign products have been invited in, Japan's mandate being that, having been opened late, it now had to hurry to catch up. The rush still continues and the compulsion to emulate results in a visible agenda which insists upon the eternal new product.

This new product, the *shinhatsubai*, does more in Japan than oil the wheels of commerce. It provides a social distraction at the same time that it promotes a kind of social cohesion. It also both contributes to and illustrates an ideology that defines cultural life. It governs means, modes, distribution, consumption and legitimation. Thus it provides 'meanings' – ideology constructs subjectivity. And strange indeed have been some of the results – supporting indeed Santayana's statement that 'fashion is something barbarous, for it produces innovation without reason and imitation without benefit.'

Edward Seidensticker has given us many an example. When pigs first arrived two hundred years ago from China they were called Nanking mice and were enormously popular, first as pets. A decade later there was a similar vogue for another exotic beast, the rabbit. By 1873, we are told, there were almost a hundred thousand in the land, all of them pets. The affection continues – even now rabbit is rarely found on Japanese menus.

Something more sartorial was the fad for squeaky shoes in the mid-nineteenth century. It was noticed that foreign footwear occasionally squeaked and it was concluded that it ought to and that any shoe which did not was inferior. Thus, an enterprising cobbler began manufacturing strips that could be inserted into new shoes. These were called 'singing leather', and it was guaranteed that this was what they did.

The attractions of sheer novelty have always been expressed overtly in Japan (in contradistinction to covertly in most of the West) and ephemerality can be a prized attribute. This tolerance, even affection for the transient, is one of the qualities of the Japanese aesthetic. Traditional Japan has long seen and shown the beauty of the ephemeral.

'If man were never to fade away . . . but lingered on forever in the world, how things would lose their power to move us. The most precious thing in life is its uncertainty.' These words by Yoshida Kenko in his *Essays in Idleness*, written in the 1330s, have been endlessly echoed. Here is Lafcadio Hearn's later take: 'For impermanency is the nature of things . . . and regret is vanity.'

Fads and fashions thus properly overtake each other like waves washing upon a beach. Each lasts for its time and then fades or – occasionally – manages to stay longer, to become institutionalized – at which point it is fashion no longer but tradition.

Visitors to Japan sometimes complain about being so constantly exposed to the latest. This is because the latest comes from wherever they come from and they are hoping for something more Japanese. Whatever it is that vexes them will, however, shortly become Japanese, at least for a time, but such innovations spoil the hoped for traditional aspect. Indeed, old Japan is now much less visible since there is so much less of it, and new Japan is now continually in your face since there is so much more of it. You go to see a pagoda and you bring back a pokemon.

Yet this dynamic is nothing new. It has been going on for a very long time, though perhaps not in so decided a manner. Motivated by an ideological conformism which originally may have been governmentally ordered but eventually became personally internalized, most Japanese seek for an individuality which is at the same time compatible with their social roles. In this they are no different from anyone else since all of us attempt it. And like everywhere else the means are sought elsewhere – outside ourselves.

Let us look at just one of the means through which an individuality is created within safe social limits – Society satisfied yet self-assured. We of the West call it being cool, chilling out. According to Dick Pountain and David Robins, scholars of the phenomenon, 'Cool is an oppositional attitude adopted by individuals or small groups to express defiance to authority – a permanent state of private rebellion.' At the same time cool forms part of a series of negotiation 'about becoming an individual while still being accepted into a group'. This is because while open rebellion invites punishment, cool 'hides its defiance behind a wall of ironic detachment, distancing itself from the source of authority rather than directly confronting it.' It is an attitude which encompasses, as Roland Barthes has phrased it, a whole 'vocabulary of detachment'.

To be cool is to be hip, with it, aware of things other than the common morality of one's class. Most civilizations contain this thin but important layer and Japan is no exception. In the Edo period the cool and the hip was called *iki*. It was a form of aesthetic self-consciousness which, like cool, took the shape of an attitude. Scholars have used the following terms to define it: sharp, straightforward, cooly gallant, resisting all compromise and conciliation, at the same time possessing a sense of charm, an allure which was also unpretentious, all high-class airs discouraged, a seeming unconcern. It was admiringly described in the *sharebon* novelettes of the Edo period and was seen in the popular woodblock prints.

One of the qualities of *iki* was (resembling a similar attitude of cool) indifference. Playing it cool was a part of *iki* decorum. Barthes could have been describing it when he wrote of cool's detachment, its sang-froid, 'the residue of a tragic movement which manages to identify gesture and action within the slenderest volume. Any cool asserts that only silence is effective.'

This was to be defined against a perceived opposite. In Edo times this was the *yabo* (the bumpkin) or the *hankatsu* (the horny). Nowadays this purveyor of ultimate cool would be defined against the *otaku* (nerd). If brought to a kind of perfection this ultimately cool person was a *tsu*, a connoisseur, someone who knew his (more rarely her) way around, who could play in the tea houses without losing his heart, who kept his emotions under control.

Many were the guides published to lead the way and to define just what being *iki* meant. Among the many categorizations of the period was the following: women (usually courtesans) considered *iki* by their customers had to have an *iki*-like face with a small nose and mouth, an exceptionally clear skin, a slim body with not much padding, hands small and expressive but not too much so since gestures had to be inconspicuous but meaningful – the kind of women seen in the late woodblock prints. She was best dressed in such *iki* colours as brown, ivory, or shades of indigo or grey, the material being either thin cotton or old silk – nothing flashier than that.

Not that there were not anomalies. In darkest Tokugawa, during the depths of national isolation, there were still foreign fads – things like calicoes, originally brought in as lowly sugar sacks, later transformed into elegant checked kimono fabrics, eventually elevated to the ultimate of conservative good taste.

In tracing the *iki* image the commentator Kaori Shoji has found this ultimate in the tea ceremony, where the master is the embodiment of the ethos: the restraint, the lack of all merely civic concern, the plain simplicity, the arcane restraint necessary. On the way there, however, there were many other *iki* considerations.

Fashion for example. Then as now fashions played a large part in commerce. Men as well as women had their perimeters. Some colours were in and some were out. Everything, however, had to express an attitude – just as it does now. The Kabuki actor Danjuro VII wore a costume with symbols and characters spelling out the word *kamawanu*, which would mean in contemporary language something like 'Couldn't Care Less'. Instant fad – this amount of cool attitudinizing being irresistible.

Irresistible not only to the new-rich upwardly mobile, the still discriminated against non-samurai merchant class – the people who most cared about *iki* – but also to the layers of home industries which created the *iki* look. As Pountain and Robins have noted, 'the cliquey solidarity implicit in cool made possible sophisticated new strategies for brand differentiation . . . the counter-culture, far from expressing a demand for proletarian revolution, was unwittingly ushering in a new phase of capitalism.'

This was as true then, in old Edo, as it is in modern Tokyo. Kimono weavers, printmakers, fan artists, publishers, all prospered as they created things to support the *iki* ethos. Danjuro's sloganed kimono may be compared with various contemporary quasi-rebellious T-shirt messages. 'Who Gives a Shit?' (in English) is one recently viewed stretched across the breast of a young person.

The rebellion is slogan-thin, it is an attitude, and yet it contains something like *iki* cool. Now it is 'casual wear' by Uniqlo (short for 'unique clothing'), stone-washed jeans, cashmere 'lumberjack' shirts, designer camouflage outfits, the expensive 'poor' look – all rural and proletariat gear become consumer items in the creation of the *iki*-like (all high-class airs discouraged) contemporary image.

The clodhopper for those who never hopped a clod illustrates Thorstein Veblen's observation that the affectation of the proletariat is a sign of moral decadence but it is also an indication that 'conspicuous consumption of valuable goods is a means of reputability to the gentleman of leisure'.

The creation of fashionable image as a prime commercial ploy is thus seen at its most spectacular in Japan. Brand names and slogans are so ubiquitous that one retailer (Seibu) made money by launching Mujirushi, a brand name meaning 'no brand', everything in the very *iki*-like colour of beige.

Even in an area as seemingly liberated as cool it is obvious that a degree of social control is implied by the very fact that *iki* is perceived as (however refined) rebellion. Ideology is inextricably related to any question of meaning. Language (verbal, visual) always mediates understanding and Japan's fads and fashions can best be understood as expressions of a concerned ideology. No more so than elsewhere, perhaps, but much more visible.

This collection of essays then may be read as investigations into the facets of this commercial image – fads, fashions, style – and as an appreciation of the meanings inherent. It could be called an attempt at a hermeneutics of the fashionable, a social limb which has been firmly seized by the arm of enterprise.

The Image Industry

Though most countries now have highly evolved image cultures, Japan's seems more noticeable, perhaps because it is more commercialized than many. Its use of image in fashion, graphics, packaging, advertisement and all forms of entertainment is indeed sometimes startling. Perhaps consequently, though the reliance on image rather than thought is everywhere a definition of modern culture, it sometimes seems as though no other place has carried this reliance to further extremes than Japan.

But let us define our terms. I take it that an image is an imitation, representation or similitude of any person or thing, sculpted, drawn, painted or otherwise made perceptible to the sight, a visual representation or reproduction: form, aspect, appearance, cast, likeness, semblance – all qualities suggested by Noah Webster.

As to a definition of the manner in which images are perceived, I would agree with Edmund Feldman that 'people see images not things. The sensations of light falling on retina are transmitted as energy impulses to the brain, where they are almost simultaneously translated into a meaningful entity called an image . . . perception is a function of the mind. We cannot experience sensation without characterizing it in some way, giving it a label, loading it with meaning. An image therefore can be defined . . . as the result of endowing optical sensations with meaning.'

Also, as Barthes has postulated, excessive use of image has resulted in 'a simple equivalence between what is seen and what is', something which (under the guise of common sense) can lead to the creation of an object, a thing, can lead to reducing being into having, can, in short, succumb to 'the disease of thinking in essences'.

Some reasons have been suggested for Japan's extreme affinity with this image-making process. One of these maintains that the nature of the written language predicates this disposition, that the *kanji*, the Chinese ideographs, are in themselves images and are so used by the Japanese, Vietnamese and South Koreans (*kanji* are no longer used in North Korea) as well as the Chinese.

Each *kanji* character symbolizes a single idea. They are logographs in that one character sometimes represents both the meaning and the sound of an entire word. In other languages (those constructed in the manner of an alphabet) a repertoire of images is neither required nor possible. Here a certain combination creates a formula – d-o-g = dog, a 'translated' image of the animal name. The same thing occurs in *kanji*, except that there is no middle step; 犬 at once becomes *quan* (*chu'uan*) in Chinese, *ken* or *inu* in Japanese. No 'translation' is necessary.

Or, as Frederick Schodt has put it, in discussing *manga* cartoons, 'the Japanese are predisposed to more visual forms of communication owing to their writing system. Calligraphy . . .

might be said to fuse drawing and writing. The individual ideograph . . . is a simple picture that represents a tangible object or an abstraction concept, emotion, or action . . . in fact, a form of cartooning.'

Certainly the idea of the cartoon is no less ancient in Japan than elsewhere, and the many surviving examples are accorded a respect not to be found in cultures which would label such efforts as primitive. The history of cartooning in Japan is indeed said to have begun among the higher rather than the lower classes. During the Heian period (794–1185), the *oko-e*, a kind of comic drawing, was popular as a hobby of the aristocracy.

The more common Japanese term for such (usually) comic images is *manga*, purportedly coined by the woodblock artist Hokusai in 1814 but only recently in common use: perhaps because only recently has there been a need for it. In Hokusai's time the popularity of such images was nowhere so great as it is now. Since the Second World War, image-driven *manga* publications have become so popular and so powerful that one critic could with perfect confidence say that 'the flourishing of a "comic culture" is one of the significant features of mass culture in present-day Japan'.

It is no accident that the *manga* explosion occurred in Japan during the mid-1950s, just at the time when, for the majority, the home TV set was becoming a possibility. It was, I think, the images on the tube that created the audience for that portable TV monitor, the *manga*. The technological assumptions of both are close.

Both insist that, as Robert MacNeil has said of American television, 'bite-sized is best, that complexity must be avoided, that nuances are dispensable, that qualifications impede the simple message, that visual stimulation is a substitute for thought, and that verbal precision is an anachronism.'

Further, 'television favours moods of conciliation and is at its best when substance of any kind is muted.' This would be yet another reason for the instant acceptance of and reliance upon television in Japan, a country where conciliation is a national stance.

In discourses which are conducted through visual imagery rather than words, a kind of one-sided conversation in images is created. It is a swift conversation, one with not much time for thought. The average length of the TV shot is under four seconds. What viewers watch are pictures (eventually millions of them) of short duration and dynamic variety. As MacNeil has written: 'It is in the nature of the medium that it must suppress the content of ideas in order to accommodate the requirements of visual interest.'

This, of course, does not trouble the viewer. Indeed it speeds him on his or her way. After all, words need to be understood while images need only to be recognized. In an image culture words become irrelevant. As Bruce Willis is reported to have stated upon reading an unfavourable critique of one of his films: 'Those [reviews] are only for people who read . . . the printed word has become a dinosaur.'

Bruce is right. Something is occurring which does indeed affect individuals, and consequently society and the culture itself. Ernst Cassirer noted as early as 1956 that 'physical reality seems to recede in proportion as man's symbolic activity advances. Instead of dealing with the things themselves man is in a sense constantly conversing with himself . . . he cannot see or know anything except by the interposition of [an] artificial medium.'

That image culture is destructive to print culture is apparent. In addition, the form in which ideas are expressed will affect

what those ideas are. There is now in Japan, as elsewhere, such a massive audience for images that a highly profitable industry has evolved. It is this which will seek to further the aims of an even more extensive image culture. It favours those assumptions and ideas it requires, it deletes those it does not. How it shows you something determines what is shown.

One example is the computer game (both in the home and in the game centre) and the various simulcra to which these have given rise. We step here from the 'real' to the 'virtual' image. An image, however, is always read as an image; the difference is merely one of degree.

Video games are usually adventure stories of some sort, or sports simulcra, or contain mysteries to be unravelled. And most of these use elementary technology and the images tend to be of similar construction. Japan has long held the lead in these image entertainments and so it is not surprising that new technology is now being developed to create a new kind of image. Among these developments has been the appearance of the virtually real person.

An example is a seventeen-year-old female high school student named Fujisaki Shiori, originally a character in a video game called *Tokimeki Memoriaru* (Memorial for a Throbbing Heart), the goal of which is to get Shiori to date the player and then fall in love with him. Packaged on compact discs, she is available to everyone but responds differently to different stimuli. The idea is to make the heart icon 'beat' more rapidly.

The game first appeared in 1994 and has now sold over a million copies. One plays until Shiori says 'I love you'. Then the game ends. Or before. Those who play say that rejection is much easier to take from a machine.

One game developer said that with games he could do things

he could not ordinarily do, such as telling a girl that he liked her. Another young man, twenty-one, is famous for having fallen in love with her. He has bought all the calendars, posters and watches that carry her picture. When she is seen in 'personal appearances' via big video screens, he appears in the audience. He has, as he says, given his heart to a virtual girl.

With this kind of success there are now plans to make virtual reality idols – entertainers in the form of computer graphics. Quasi-females without the encumbrances of stories, plots or games, they will be able to sing and dance at least as well as some of the real ones, will never get tired, and are, by definition, cheap dates.

Among those already on the market is Jenni (Jenny), product of Digital Media Lab, affiliated with Mitsubishi Electric Company. She is the child of a Japanese mother and an Arab father, is fluent in both Japanese and English and is skilled at singing and dancing. She also appears on an Internet karaoke service. Another virtual girl is Kyoko Date, a product of Hori Pro, Inc., and already out on compact disc. She has a radio programme as well, and her radio voice is heard on her CD. She, like all the others, is created through something called Motion Capture. Scores of personal computers are connected to infrared light cameras that register the motions of many small plastic balls placed on a real, human, dancer. And, of course, there is Fujisaki Shiori, shortly dropping her date game, and available on a CD from Konami Co.

The *Asahi Shimbun* welcomed these simulated creatures in an editorial. The DK96 project at Hori Productions, it said, is to create a girl who can dance and sing, has sex appeal, but is also thoughtful in that she can deliver lines in several languages. The DK96 members say they are confident and mention the highly successful computer-dinosaurs in *Jurassic Park*.

Though 'live' appearance will not be possible, she will not be choosy about work, 'even if she has to take on two or three assignments at the same time', and she will be put through the same procedures that are used to promote human idols.

First, write-ups in the entertainment columns will be secured, then pictures in the graphic magazines. The 'handshake session' might be difficult, but DK96 thinks this can be managed somehow. Then there are 'personal' appearances on big outdoor screens and, though she will cost a lot to create, one may always, they say, get back one's costs by making her appear in television commercials.

An even more cost-effective image-industry innovation is a recent Bandai Networks offering, *Meru de Koishite* (Love via E-mail), in which the users can exchange e-mail with one of several virtual women of various ages and occupations. Their goal is to win the 'love' of the chosen women, a task requiring about ninety e-mail messages.

The game itself lasts for one month. At the end the player receives one of two final messages. 'You are just a friend' means he has lost. 'I love you very much' tells him that he is a winner. Launched in 2000, over 300,000 males have signed up so far.

The image-game is highly detailed (some of the 'women' do not want to receive e-mail during their 'working hours'), so much so that some subscribers have actually contacted Bandai Networks to ask how they can meet these women. With this kind of interest being generated, Bandai has now introduced a new virtual love game. This one caters for women and is called *Watashi no Oojisama* (My Prince).

Just how lucrative image-aids can be is indicated by the earlier success of the Tamagotchi, a virtual pet, the fame of which reached even foreign shores. It was a compact, portable computer game shaped like an egg (*tamago*) which you 'watch' (*gotchi* being a kind of homonym for the English word). Though now dead as the dodo, the Tamagotchi was once the image choice of up to half of the population of Japan.

The instructions read: 'You take care of Tamagotchi, the mysterious small animal on the liquid crystal screen. The special feature is that Tamagotchi will grow up in diverse ways, depending on how you raise it.' The computer image of an egg gave birth five seconds after a button was pushed. The creature had a life expectancy of a week or so and during this time constantly called for attention with a beeping sound. The owner was required to feed it, to dispose of its excrement, to play with it, and to discipline it – all by pushing various buttons. Its appearance and character was affected by the degree of care it received. If not fed enough it might die of starvation; if ignored it turned delinquent. There were ways to make it old (an *oyajichi*, with features of the aged) and it could always be reprogrammed to start all over again.

There were Internet pages which offered advice on how to make it reach an advanced age (discipline it and feed it less, no matter how much it complained); there was also dissident advice on how to kill the thing as quickly and efficiently as possible.

Invented by a toy-manufacturer who was pondering the mingling of pets with toys, Tamagotchi became popular at once. Released at the end of 1996, it sold millions of units and half a year later was still being eagerly awaited by would-be buyers. These were initially teenage girls but eventually the audience included everyone. Tamagotchi, the pet image, had attained the dimensions of a craze.

In addition the baby bird was vended as the logo for various products and was animated for advertisement on the tube as well. As an image, Tamagotchi thus displayed differences from its parents – digital games. It was not entirely presentational, it presumed a dialogue. The cute little encoded avians had to be cared for. This, said some educators (as well as the Bandai Co. Ltd, which made it), was a good thing. In the cities the young are not allowed pets, they do not learn the interdependence so necessary for a healthy society. Tamagotchi teaches them responsibility.

Some owners, it was optimistically said, develop a parental attachment to the chick that is as deep as that toward human offspring. On television a doctor, a grown man, said that when his passed away he was sadder than when one of his patients died. An Internet home page displayed illustrations of Tamagotchi tombstones and invited people to send valedictions to be engraved on them.

There were other reasons for the popularity, however. Teenagers in all countries are notoriously under-empowered. Their entire culture is about ways to acquire an adult endowment before their time. With the tiny chick they finally had something completely under their thumbs. It survived through their decision, its death was their whim. Indeed, it lived the kind of life they think they do, but it could do nothing about it. They could. They had Tamagotchi.

That it become a craze is perhaps indicative also of something other than mere popularity. In Japan more than in some countries everyone is supposed to look the same. If a new fashion is evolved (*chapatsu* – dyed hair – loose socks on girls, portable phones, Burberry scarves, and *puri-cura* – print club – tiny stickers of one and one's friends, all beaming and holding up V-sign fingers), then if you do not have it, you are not in but out. But even if you have it, there are more crazes inside crazes. For a time only the white Tamagotchi really counted. Other colours were somehow inferior.

In Japan, land of instant commercial enthusiasms, the computerized avian went the way of earlier products. But now that the image industry is more heavily motivated by commercial success and, consequently, growth, one fad leads to another. As the commentator Mark Thompson has said: ' . . . it's not surprising that Tamagotchi is being derided as yet another fad . . . but that's too easy. The possibilities of virtual pets are too rich. First-generation Tamagotchi probably won't last another year, but as a concept it will most definitely evolve into a dominant theme.'

And so it has: robots are now evolved to the extent that marketing is being envisioned. Aibo, the faux-canine devised by Sony in 1999, can now be trained to play ball as well as wag its tail. It has, says the catalogue, voice-recognition skills and six 'emotions', and it is understood that the creature requires no house training. Though its image as a 'pet' is strong, Sony – perhaps remembering what happened to that other animal friend, Tamagotchi – is playing this down, insisting upon calling the beast 'entertainment'.

Next in line is the humanoid robot, named Asimo, which made its debut in 2000. He (there is no she, even on the drawing boards), like all consumer electronics, supposed 'to make our lives easier'. Indeed both *manga* and *anime* are full of robots who 'help mankind', and Japan has a long history of the *karakuri*, those mechanical dolls which were ingeniously made in the Edo period and designed to roll helpfully over the *tatami* and bring cups of tea.

Asimo's duties are now vague, but 'helping' is certainly among them. He is marketed as friendly, and the buyer who acquires him is supposed to match this amicable stance. You are not to 'purchase' such a humanoid, you are to 'adopt' it. Certainly Honda is wary of creating any servant image. An official went so far as to say that it was only in other countries that the robot was turned into the valet or the butler, that Japan's apprehension was different. In Japan, Asimo is seen as a machine that 'loves and serves' humans. They are more like friends and, unlike Hal or the Matrix, would never do harm. At present they are recommended as companions for the ill, aged, and/or lonely.

The robot proved how user-friendly he was to just everyone when he rang the bell to open trading on the New York Stock Exchange on February 14, 2002. A soccer-playing robot was ready for the 2002 World Cup. Programmed to do friendly and fun things, these robots are a further extension of a trend noted earlier on the faces of mobile phones. These are programmed to meet their owners with a winking cartoon face. Pleasant, smiling, friendly – these are aspects at which the new technology is hard at work.

A nice face makes whatever it is socially acceptable, at the same time it creates a market for the pleasant, the non-threatening. And this is occurring at the very time when there is an unsatisfied market for friendly faces. In big-city Japan, people have reached New York heights of invisibility. They do not see each other. They do not want to. Anonymous smiles are rare. Hence a need for robotized ones.

The enormous commercial growth of the image industry, the overwhelming availability of such images, leads one to wonder as to the nature of the audience. I was recently told that some sixty billion pictures are taken worldwide every year. Someone is supposed to look at them – but there are not that many people in the world.

We live in such an inundating sea of images that it is a commonplace that we now look at the image and not at the thing itself. (The icon is the shutterbug in front of the famous view, putting eyepiece to eye, clicking and turning away, never having looked directly at the view photographed.)

A result is that essence is turned into surface and integrity vanishes. Photos are no longer responsible records. They are part of the new world of maximum simulation – like video-games, like television. Everything is relative and all is flattened. Which is what Cassirer was saying when he maintained that 'instead of dealing with the things themselves man is . . . constantly conversing with himself.' We have now reached an age where we may begin to appreciate the Biblical second commandment which, as you will remember, says that: 'Thou shalt not make unto thee any graven image, any likeness of any thing.'

We might also speculate as to why the image industry has been so extraordinarily successful in Japan. I have indicated some reasons but there is another as well, one which is aesthetic.

One Japanese aesthetician, Tosa Mitsuoki, early formulated a rule regarding images, the like of which would be uncommon in the West. 'If', he wrote, 'there is a painting which is lifelike and which is good for that reason, that work has followed the laws of life. If there is a painting which is not lifelike and which is good for that reason, that work has followed the laws of painting.'

This was written in the seventeenth century, and in it Tosa clearly separates, in a manner uncommon among aestheticians of other cultures, the separate identities of not only object and image but also the means of rendering it. This suggests too an awareness of the differences involved in the creation of images. He distinguishes between two kinds of images: those which mirror the object and those which mirror the mechanisms through which the image is made.

This latter concern is one which has been one of the richest sources of Japanese aesthetics – though respecting the artistic often means doing so at the expense of any more realistic style, that style which followed the 'laws of life'. This respect of 'the laws of painting' extended to other disciplines. It would retain the grain of the wood, the strata of the stone, the limitations of black ink on white paper, the syllable count of *haiku* and *waka*. These are 'good' because they have followed other than the 'laws of life'.

Images which respect the realistic limitations of pen and brush, woodblock printing, computer graphics, and the laws of virtual reality are, in this respect, the same. Illusionism or naturalistic reality, which is a major part of the Western aesthetic heritage, was never common in Japan. Mimesis, that meticulous imitation of aspects of the sensible world, was not of major importance. Indeed, what Mitsuoki meant by those works which followed the laws of life have never looked particularly lifelike to the mimetic Western viewer.

To this extent then, Japanese aesthetic theory has long insisted upon the interposition of an artificial medium – be this the grain of wood, the contrasts of the *sumi* ink painting, *Shonen Jump* or Fujisaki Shiori. There are differences but these are those of quality. Optical sensations are endowed with meaning and we may only enquire as to the value of the meaning.

Sesshu or Tamagotchi? Do those works which respect the law of art violate the integrity of their subjects? Of course they do. They are intended to. But they have other concerns. Japan is not alone in experiencing this dichotomy, but it is perhaps alone in perceiving none.

It is, then, upon this base that the image industry of Japan firmly rests. It is also from here that the industry grows. It, in addition, presents us with images which are not intended for any single individual but for everyone. In this way the image industry markets. It editorializes because its own basic image precludes all the others and insists upon a single, standardized model. It is this which it sells.

Fashion's Tongues

We all express ourselves in various ways: deeds, words, gestures, decorations. The expression is presentational – one shows who one is, or who one wishes to be taken for. One of the means is dress. A kind of visual grammar is the result. A 'statement' formed by an ensemble which 'speaks' plainly of the intentions, conscious or otherwise, of the wearer.

In Japan, a land where the emblematic is usually visible, the traditional language of dress is more codified than in some other countries. It is consequently better known and more consciously used. Yanagida Kunio, the early folklorist, has said that 'clothing is the most direct indication of a people's general frame of mind'.

If this is so, then traditional dress said much about the people wearing it. The kimono comes in only two sizes, male and female. It is rarely designed to fit the wearer. Rather, the wearer is designated, as it were, to fit it. The assumption is that, except for important sexual differences, we Japanese are all alike. This being so, tailoring as a form of uniqueness is not traditionally valued. Since harmony is our goal in all things, we show a happy similarity in our national costume.

There are, to be sure, minor variations. A young girl indicates that she is young by wearing bright colours; an older woman admits her age by wearing subdued shades. Traditionally the wealthy but otherwise unprivileged merchant showed his state by wearing a plain kimono but one lined with quite expensive materials. Also both kimono pattern and hairstyle indicate the social position of the wearer. A geisha in full ensemble would be 'read' differently than a married woman of good family.

The kimono, like all forms of dress, also shows more than it ostensibly presents. Since the language of clothing, like any other language, rests on nuance, the kimono defines the wearer in more senses than one. In contrast to the Arab kaftan or the Persian chador, clothing which has no contact with the body at all, merely covers it, the kimono delineates the wearer. It is, particularly in the woman's costume, so tight and so supported by layers of inner slips that it is like a moulded shell.

What is moulded, however, are not the breasts, the hips, the behind, those areas emphasized in the West, but the torso. The result is a costume so tight that it hobbles the wearer and prevents any actions other than walking, standing, sitting, kneeling – a repertoire of movements which, given bodily possibilities, is quite limited.

The suggestion is that something this tight and constricting must therefore enclose – like the lobster's shell – something soft and fluid. In this sense, the kimono may be seen as a metaphor for the idea that the Japanese has of herself or himself.

We are a people whose social consciousness is at least as strong as our individual consciousness. We live in a rigid, conforming society and both our strong social self and our strict social rules are necessary because otherwise we would not know who we are. Like crustaceans we are defined not by an inner core but by an outer armour, which may be social or sartorial. These – our ideas, our clothes – are informed from the outside. We so express our social self because, to an extent, that is all there is.

(There are other readings as well. Women, for example, are hobbled by the kimono because they have, to an extent, agreed to appear as chattels – frail, expensive creatures one of whose functions is to appear as items of conspicuous male consumption.)

A standard costume is like an accepted idea. It is self-evident. We do not examine its meaning until we have ceased to believe in it. In this sense, the meaning of the kimono was not apparent until it ceased being widely worn.

Now we see – a truism – that those who wear the kimono also entertain old-fashioned ideas. At the same time, there lingers about the kimono, naturally enough, an air of respectability. The well-brought up young lady owns one and wears it upon proper occasions (tea-ceremony and flower-arranging lessons, weddings, at New Year's) though the rest of the time she may be in slacks and a sweater. She is showing that though she may have modern ideas she is also a decent girl.

(She is not suggesting, I think – as would the American girl gotten out of her jeans to wear a wedding dress – that she in the garment for peripheral reasons but that her real self is different. Rather, the Japanese young woman is stating that she is both modern and respectable at the same time.)

Hers is one answer (sometimes in kimono, sometimes not) to a communicative question which the Japanese have been facing for some time. How do you sartorially indicate who you are when the means for doing so is disappearing?

The kimono was ousted by Western clothing when Japan decided to join the rest of the world after its long seclusion. During this sartorial modernization there were many mistakes – bustles worn backwards and the like – because the Japanese could not yet read the lexicon of Western dress.

As might have been expected the Japanese choice initially was for Western clothing too formal for either the occasion or the person or both. Hats, gloves, sticks – elements known originally to have had aristocratic nuances – were used by all Japanese men who could afford them. Women also were likewise too dressed up. One still sees remnants of this early reading even in informal court functions, and Japanese abroad are usually, given foreign standards, overdressed. That the Japanese in Western clothes looks always off to a wedding or a funeral is an old observation but one still valid.

One understands the reasons. The rigidity of the kimono is being sought in the rigidity of foreign formal dress. Overdressing for an occasion (which is what all formal dress consists of) means, by definition, a presentation of the social self. The clothing is much like the conversation on such occasions – social, that is, impersonal.

In the West, however, dress is now nothing if not personal and the language of fashion has broken into various dialects. Individuality is sought, if not always achieved, and formal dress has all but disappeared – you can go to the opera in a sweatshirt. And given the idealization that adults in an aging society give the young, many mature people, Americans and European, dress like unbuttoned children: snow suits for the boys, sun suits for the girls.

The Japanese, having scrapped their own native costume and having proved understandably maladroit in handling the various

nuances of Western dress, are now presented with a new problem – or rather, the same old problem under a new guise: how to present the social self given only the highly individualized clothing styles from which they must choose.

Perhaps consequently the perpetual vogue for the novel, but only that novel which can be accommodated at the same time. An example would be the *haikara* (high collar) look which evolved during the late Meiji period. High collars and other fashionable appurtenances were combined in an eclectic and even flamboyant manner. Young men of means adopted an elegant sloppiness which was eventually designated as *bankara*, the first syllable taken from a *kanji* connoting barbarism. From 'barbarian collar' it was but a step to codifying the look itself, which accommodated a whole line of 'barbarian' fashions, among the latest being the hip-hop look.

To an extent, however, choice is already made by fashion itself. The linguistic equivalent might be free speech, but the true aim is to make everyone speak alike for a season. The Japanese problem, its quest for clothing expressing a social norm, is solved so long as everyone appears more or less the same, even though the clothing itself may have originally carried personal nuances.

Jeans, for example. They have become the uniform of the young in all countries. Being a uniform, this means that, sartorially, the young are all saying the same thing. Though the fashion for jeans was originally radical in America, land of their birth (we are not going to dress up, we are egalitarian) and even to an extent revolutionary (down with elitist thought, down with civilization), it has now become the equivalent of an accepted idea. Jeans are cheap, easy to wash, do not need pressing and everyone else wears them – the accent is demotic.

In Japan, jeans became at once the new uniform of the

young. Though originally carrying connotations of 'thinking young' (and so advertised) jeans were domesticated. In a short time they (chosen a size too small and given to shrinkage besides) became the kimono equivalent. They encase snugly and safely and their message is socially conciliatory – if everyone says the same thing, then no one says anything. Jeans became the unexceptionable container for young bodies and its original, somewhat inflammatory message has now become its opposite: we are conforming, we are rocking no boats.

Not that this has not occurred in other countries, and not that other countries do not likewise seek the safety and security of an unexceptionable social costume – but the results are more visible in Japan. Also, given the admitted difficulties that many Japanese encounter in 'reading' modern fashion, mistakes occur, and these are often visible as well.

Take, for example, the emblazoned T-shirt. In America, land of its birth, wearing a Coca-Cola emblazoned T-shirt originally meant precisely that one would not subscribe to those institutionalized habits which are perceived as accompanying indiscriminate and habitual Coca-Cola drinking. The intent was ironic. The viewer was being put on, and the wearer was doing the putting – as in the wearing of surplus US Army gear, which in the USA, meant you were anti-Vietnam War and were hence anti-Army. Definition by opposites became, for a time, a part of sartorial grammar.

In Japan, however, a land unusually innocent of irony, Coca-Cola wearers love Coca-Cola. It is a sign of their modernity. And surplus Army uniform (always US, never Japanese) means merely being with-it in some (to the Japanese) obscure sense. And as for the emblazoned messages, since no one can read them or, if able to read them, understand them, the mere fact of wearing English

on a T-shirt indicates merely a contemporary and progressive frame of mind.

The mock come-on or put-down built into the American youth context is entirely missing. (Now missing in America as well, one must add. The irony of the later decades of the twentieth century did not survive into the twenty-first: the initial *Star Wars* episode was seen as a lavish, over-the-top parody of junk comics, the latest *Star Wars* episode is seen as an earnest, if juvenile, adventure story.) At the same time, however, often a message will survive the transfer and itself morph into something different.

As I write (summer 2002) the parlous state of the Japanese economy and the bellicose state of the rest of the world has resulted in a stripped-down fashion – plebeian hip-hop, thrift-store-style dresses, cyber-sneakers and camouflage pants mixed with neo-punk, the ragbag military look being enhanced by a mini-vogue for the *gutra*. This is the checked cotton scarf, usually held in place over the head with a band, associated with Arab costume.

Worn in Japan around the neck, the origin is not included in whatever slender message it carries. 'I didn't know they were Arab until I went into the shop just now and looked at the label', said one Harajuku boutique owner who affirmed that buyers did not associate them with Islam. They were associated only with current if anonymous chic, though in several stores they were called 'Afghan scarves'.

After the Gulf War sale of military jackets shot up. 'Maybe more US strikes [against Afghanistan] will lead to more military sales', opined the owner. Thus the original meaning of the *gutra* has changed from specific (Islamic) identification to a general and diffuse icon of the cool, the smart, the right now – pacifistic appropriations of military chic.

Or take, for example, the now extinct but once mildly prevalent 'too-big' American look, women in redesigned male clothing purposely several sizes too large, pants or skirt bunched at the belt, coat or blouse sleeves extending down over the fingers, shoulders sagging because too wide. Its message was that the girl in the too-large male suit was really saying that, try as she may for a man's role in this man's world (now that she has been 'liberated' enough to attempt it), the part is still just 'too big' for her.

This message may have had some slight relevance in the USA where there had been an amount of publicity concerning women's presumed liberation, but in Japan, where woman was scarcely liberated at all, the message had no social relevance. It was a message without a context.

In America the implication was that the woman wearing this outfit and so obviously failing to perform the male role was, therefore, a figure of some fun. At the same time she was plucky. As she might herself have said, she was dancing as hard as she could. She (Diane Keaton in *Annie Hall*) thus became attractive, a person who admits her faults. She was 'smart', 'cool', adjectives incorporating some degree of honesty and charm. She was also safe, since she had none of the threat of the Women's Libber about her – she was, in fact, a turncoat, snuggling up to and affirming the male image. In Japan, where the outfit promptly arrived with all the publicity given any new fashion from abroad, this wealth of nuance was lost. The too-big look was simply taken over, unexamined. Once it was looked at, however, it underwent a transformation. Though girls did not take to it, boys did. The message happened to coincide, USA/Japan, but there was a gender change.

Boys in bunched and baggy trousers cannot fill father's pants. Though they are dancing as hard as they can, they really

can't make it in the corporate world of their parents. Both costume and the social responsibility it suggests is just 'too much'. This large outfit is, in Japan, revealed as nothing other than the dark blue serge suit long associated with the orderly and conservative life. (There is no hippie costume which is 'too big', and in Japan the idea of a kimono 'too large' would carry no meaning at all.) The outsize ensemble is just like Papa's best suit and it means that Sonny cannot live up to inherited responsibilities.

Here the effect was consciously 'funny', and young men so dressed were figures of fun, though in both countries 'funny' was to be read as 'disarming' in that, like all joke outfits, this one really sets out to placate. Also, it ends up affirming the virtues it set out to criticize.

Later, in that mindless way fashions have, this too-large look attached itself to another foreign fashion which had, originally at any rate, a few critical ambitions of its own. This was the American hip-hop fashion, young blacks wearing sports clothes with pants pulled to groin level and baseball caps on backward. Originally a uniform of mild dissent (we're not gonna dress up for you) it became, in Japan, a continuation of the just-can't-keep-up Diane Keaton look – though it was naturally entirely reserved for young Japanese males.

Thus for a season boys showed their belly buttons and exposed a fringe of pubic hair in a society which is, more than most, uptight about such public display. Any affront to 'public decency' was nullified, however, both by the juvenile nature of the costume and by that fact that neither wearer nor viewer knew that the style had originally meant to criticize those not wearing it. If the young Japanese hip-hopper knew that he was copying an ethnic style designed to create a tribal identity, he knew it only as 'fashion' – so complete is style detached from content.

Though the messages of fashion sometimes coincide between the West and Japan, most often they do not. Take, for example, the American ensemble which consisted of highly unfashionable materials such as georgette and velveteen cut in a deliberately old-fashioned manner (puffed sleeve, yoke neck) and often accompanied by hair in a bun, or a primped perm, and sometimes granny-glasses.

This very short-lived post-hippie fashion implied that 'we thinking young American females are so serious that we do not care for fashion – we have found our true values, those of our grandparents, and we are sober and honest enough to proclaim this'. Such a complicated sartorial metaphor is not legible in Japan where, in any event, the strata of historical Western costume are unknown. Still, since fashion is fashion, this look was everywhere in Tokyo and the larger cities for a time.

Here again, however, some changes were made. Though Japan has seen many a fashion downgraded, there is, at the same time, a tendency to hold on to some. Even the kimono is, at certain times and places, proper and hence fashionable still. In any event, there is no need for ironic fashion-mongering. The Japanese thus saw the unfashionable look as a continuation of one of their own fashions: the velvet-ribboned little-girl dress, which has never gone out of fashion for certain little girls.

Styles of the 1930s, to which this ensemble was in the USA most beholden, were, in Japan, not recognized as such and, in any event, the implied nostalgia could not be felt. It is not that Japan cannot be nostalgic, but in fashion it is more often nostalgic about someone else's nostalgia – references to juke-boxes, duck's-ass hairstyles, Elvis, and the rest. None of this is connected with Japan as it is – it is nostalgia once removed.

Consequently no mixed-messages were detected and Kate Greenaway was laid directly on top of Clyde's Bonnie.

A reason for the illiterate nature of Japanese importation is that the various interfaces of fashion are different. As explained by one designer: 'Fashion in Europe and the USA is structured in a top-to-bottom hierarchy because famous designers like Christian Dior release a season's collection and set the trends. But in Japan it's the opposite – fashions originate on the street and ascend to midstream.' To which fashion-commentator Kate Drake adds that there are no seasons (in the Dior sense), 'only tsunami-sized fashion trends that breeze through in weeks, months – whatever'.

This is true and to get them there someone has to push. When the Portuguese first arrived in Japan during the sixteenth century the fashions were aped at once and whole native workshops, counterfeiting cloaks, breeches, plumed hats, sprang up. The merchants of Edo were inspired by (or perhaps themselves inspired) Kabuki actors who promoted lines of dress much as TV entertainers still do. But now there is an entire hierarchy controlling Japanese fashion on its way upward. The sales level sets the pitch and the upper levels refine and reinterpret. This amount of editorialization on the important item argues for a degree of need.

Not only do the Japanese read Western fashion differently (jeans), or creatively (the too-big suit on boys), and wrongly (the '30s granny look), they are also not at all comfortable with imported fashion and never have been – perhaps therefore the near-incredible rate of change. As Drake has noted of fashion in Japan: 'A brand can go from unknown to saturation in a month'.

The only Western dress to which Japanese have thoroughly accustomed themselves, and which they wear in a natural manner, is the institutionalized uniform. We foreigners are always surprised at this because we are used to seeing it only in specialized professions – nurses, stewardesses etc. – where typically the wearers are female.

In Japan, however, the institutional costume is everywhere. All Japanese cooks wear a 'cook suit', white with a big, puffed hat; most younger Japanese students wear the black serge high-collared Prussian schoolboy suit; day-labourers concoct typical outfits from rubber-soled socks, pegged pants, cummerbunds. Even ordinary men or women off for a day of skiing or hiking fit themselves out in full skiing or hiking ensemble. The conclusion is inescapable. Japanese are truly at home with Western dress only if it is some form of livery.

Someone has written that to wear livery is to be 'editorialized, censored', which is quite true. But it is also to be finally, happily, defined. It is this need for definition (even at the price of editorialization and censorship) which seems so felt by the modern Japanese.

The need is universal (hence the concept of fashion at all, everyone wearing the same thing at the same time, finally for the time being defined) but, as always, it is more visible in Japan. Everyone sheds his or her jeans only to step into his or her blue serge suit or skirt, and the company badge completes the outfit.

To be defined is to know who you are, socially, even sociologically. This, in Japan, is of unusual importance. Thus fashions in which everyone 'says' the same thing. Thus this 'conversation' using only the safest of clichés. If 'who I am' is the sartorial statement the world over, then clothes can also answer the question of 'who am I?' The Japanese response to this is: 'I am what I appear to be; I am the function that I am dressed for.'

There are thus, within a purely Japanese context, no problems of ambiguity, dishonesty, irony, or even intention versus interpretation (terms often used in speaking of a possible vocabulary of dress). Likewise, since the costume that even the young must eventually opt for is so unequivocal, there is no room for eloquence, wit, or even any but the most rudimentary information.

Unexampled similarity remains the ideal of Japanese dress. Even radical differences must be standardized. As has been noted of the fad for different coloured hair: 'Nowadays, if you don't colour your hair, *you're* the one who's different.' Extending this into global terms is Befu Harumi's exegesis of the two aspects of Japan's self-definition. One is for export: 'The Japanese, by virtue of their sameness, are different.' The other is for domestic consumption: 'In spite of our differences we are all the same.'

Kawaii – Kingdom of the Cute

Acres of wide-eyed little girls, aisles of cuddly animals, screens full of cute little monsters, all in kindergarten colours; adults read kids' comic books in train and subway, banks give small stuffed pandas to grown-up clients; the Liberal Democratic Party had a 'Ryu-doll' for its voters and they voted in former Prime Minister Hashimoto Ryutaro; Hello Kitty regards us from every counter, and Walt Disney in all his protean forms is ambassador extraordinary – one cannot, in Japan, escape from the cartoon, the comic-book atmosphere, the cute.

Cute (*kawaii*) is variously defined. Webster's says it means 'attractive by reason of daintiness or picturesqueness in manners or appearance, as a child or a small animal', and the *Oxford English Reference Dictionary* offers 'affectedly attractive'. Certainly *kawaii* means all this. But in Japan it also means more. As Rebecca Mead has informed us:

> The cute look is said to signify an assertion of

independence on the part of the young women who adopt it, since, rather than simply putting on an ensemble presented to them by a designer, they are creating their own whimsical outfits and giving their inventiveness free rein. There's a popular magazine in Japan called *Cutie*, which offers hints on how to make one's person and environment *more cute*: a recent feature suggests sticking red heart-shaped cutouts all over your toilet seat.

In the West we are admonished by the highest authority to 'put away childish things'. In Japan, however, as a newspaper editorial recently stated: 'Experts consistently point to the importance of cuteness in the Japanese value system. Cuteness is considered to be good and a virtue. Unlike their counterparts in the United States and Europe, youth in Japan feels less pressure to grow out of childhood and rush into adulthood.'

This innocent rectitude is important to those Japanese still influenced by a Confucian-based insistence upon goodness and integrity. One of the creators of PostPet Software has remarked that 'there is a tendency to regard a childish spirit as more virtuous than maturity. That is why adults surround themselves with cute things.'

There have been a number of explanations for this prevalence for the cute. One is geographical. With land prices so high and people so many, space is at a premium. Miniaturization has proved a kind of answer. Architect Richard Rogers has said that this leads to 'building a 20 x 20 foot building 12 storeys high', and a result – tiny shops, minuscule bars, capsule hotels – is that Tokyo's coming more and more to resemble an adult Kiddy Land. One that comes equipped with miniature merchandizing

– a tool chest that fits in the pocket, the world's smallest watch, and lots of tiny affectedly attractive stuffed animals. Smaller – and cuter – is better.

Another explanation blames (or praises) women. The critics point out that fashions for the infantile are not purchased by infants but by young adults, female ones. According to the Sanrio Company (the Korean concern that created Hello Kitty) 'the items sold to Japanese girls between five and getting married would be bought in the USA only by girls from four to seven years old'. True, and at the same time the cries of 'kawaii' coming from women customers really mean 'cool' or 'neat'. It 'does not necessarily imply childishness – it also means "I like it" or even "I'll buy it".'

Making and selling things *kawaii* is an enormous industry and it is driven by women who buy it. But why are such things ('character goods' as they are called in the industry) sold in such large numbers. A senior analyst at the research section of the largest of the manufacturers said that he believed 70 per cent of those he had surveyed really sought solace in character products, and that the more stressed out they were, the more strongly attached they were to the items.

In the survey, 84 per cent of the respondents (aged seven to 69, 55 per cent men, 73 per cent women) said they owned at least one character product, and nearly half said they owned twenty or more. Sato Noriko, reporting on the results, said that Bandai was surprised that ownership among the older people was so high. 'It shows how character products have permeated into all age groups', he said. And, perhaps, how stressed all of them are.

The stress might be alleviated because cuteness 'communicates power relations and power plays, effectively combining weakness, submission and humility with influence, domination

and control'. The words are those of Brian McVeigh, who goes on to find that cuteness itself is feminine, childish and submissive, but that it at the same time reflects authority.

Here an example might be cuteness as displayed in action – the presentation of the Japanese family on the TV tube. While there is home drama galore and tears for the entire family on all of the many soap-opera serials devoted to the family, during the commercials the families are always happy, often manically so.

Here is an example from a pre-processed noodle product advertisement. Father and kids are expectantly seated at the family table while mother triumphantly pours hot water into the styrofoam cup. The odour is noted with wide smiles and father, carried away by expectant glee, actually compliments his wife on her buying prowess. '*Sasuga*', he says to her ('Isn't that just like you'), smacking his lips and beaming. She simpers her pleasure and the children grimace and look at each other knowingly – everything is OK with Mom and Dad.

Messages are rife in this small vignette. Among things suggested are: buying the right thing is the true secret of a happy home life; a woman is fulfilled through her mercantile choice; male regard is earned through proper product identification. There are some unintended messages as well. The family is insane – they behave like manic-depressives in the upward phase. Yet everything is benign. In being happy with the product the family has reached a higher harmony. No dissent, no confrontation will rend this happy accord. And in behaving like a demented mouse family, this social unit has shown that they are equally unexceptional, that they are really Mr and Mrs Status Quo and all their little Quos. That they are, in fact, no threat.

The message is so incessant on Japanese television and so accounts for the tone of the medium that one begins to see the

presentation of the unexceptional as one of the ingredients of *kawaii*. All the adults in this televised ad are really children. They cock their heads like precocious youngsters, they use the gesture of the schoolchild, they smile and laugh in an infantile fashion. Further, the disembodied voice we hear is plainly an adult imitating a child. In addition, the music accompanying this is reminiscent of the jaunty marches associated, in Japan at any rate, with kindergarten.

Perhaps behind this is some urge to return to the golden age of undisciplined, permissive, Japanese childhood, but the implication would seem rather to be that we are all as harmless as children. Look at us: we make fools of ourselves, we invite you to laugh at us, and yet we are so harmless that your laughter cannot but be indulgent, that your hand cannot but reach into your billfold. The cute is commercialized. I am a small child (or a small animal), I am affectedly attractive.

Further, the personification (Hello Kitty) is simplified to an extreme. Social critic Takeda Toru has written that the success of Hello Kitty and Pokemon does not rest upon mere cuteness. He suggests that 'the simplified, often stylised, appearance of Japanese character products (very different from Disney's characters, with their human expressions suggesting deep feelings) fits the communication pattern of today's youth.' These offer no opportunity for reciprocity (Hello Kitty has no mouth). The young may impose their own fantasies on these creatures. Indeed, they fit youth because they do not have characteristics. Nor do the young, not yet. Character productions thus have no character. If they occasionally express amiability, this is because that quality is chosen.

Perhaps the pervading juvenility of so much Japanese popular culture is the result of conciliatory intentions. The fatuity of the cute is intentional, its bland, inane foolishness is a small price to pay when the result is complete uniformity and utter consistency.

To the foreign observer, to be sure, the view brings to mind Douglas MacArthur's famous and much resented description of the Japanese as a nation of twelve-year-olds. Looking closer, the contemporary foreigner is apt to sense that the General missed the age by at least a decade. But my argument is not that the Japanese themselves are really like this. Rather, that the image they project, that they choose to present, is this. And that there are reasons (some of them given above) for this and that the more one regards the phenomenon the more one can learn from it

Take, for example, that major manufacturing machine for cute-making, the Purikura. This is a digital photo booth that, within moments, produces a small page of coloured photo stickers. The name is derived from Print Club, English making *kawaii* things even more *kawaii*. In Japanese this comes out Purinto Kurabu and (due to the national passion for shortening, compressing, making small) results in Purikura.

Up to five people can crowd around it and have their photos taken. If they want, they can also be photographed against or amid various digital frames. These often contain such cute cartoon figures as that big blue cat named Doraemon, Atom Boy, Hello Kitty, and such virtual visitors from abroad as Mickey and Minnie Mouse. Or there are 'idol' pop singers (Amuro Namie or Celine Dion) or youth-cult faves (singing group Kinki Kids or American actor Keanu Reeves) for group celebrity photo opportunities. 'Cute' poses are adopted (for years the standard has been a great big smile and the right arm extended with the index and middle fingers spread in the V-sign) and the picture is taken.

When it emerges from the machine the page of coloured stickers, sixteen to a sheet is common, are divided among those photographed. Scissors are attached to the booth anticipating just this need. The individual pictures have various uses: decoration on portable phones, use on letters and postcards or (overwhelmingly) careful placement in small, portable, plastic albums.

These are carried about by the girls (few boys bother) and have a number of uses. One is that the album constitutes proof that the owner belongs to a specific group, not just those with whom she has her photo taken, but also that much larger group that endorses Print Club – the album is a statement of identity.

At the same time is also a statement of popularity. Look at me becomes look at us, as Richard Chalfen and Mai Murui discovered in their investigations into Purikura. They were told by one young informant: 'The more I have the more comfortable I feel about my relations with others . . . that [album] is proof that I have lots of friends.' Purikura stickers are a medium for pasting people to one another.

The means is the machine but, since the users are usually pre-teen females, the medium itself is the cute – the small, the inoffensive, the affectedly attractive, as in a child or a small animal. As a means of empowering the powerless, the legions of the cute defend and at the same time wield a market-place authority. This strength manifests itself in more cute products until the landscape is filled with them. If one cannot escape from the candied and the cartooned in Japan, it is because they have already occupied the place.

The Sex Bazaar

All societies have, to an extent, discovered in the sex lives of their citizens a powerful incentive to commerce. Indeed, even left to itself sex tends toward commercialization. How much more useful, then, if this lucrative urge can be channelled to more effective mercantile use.

This idea is one that occurs to any businessman, and my discussing Japan's achievements in the field here should not be seen as finding the Japanese phenomenon in any way unique. Rather, as always, Japan's way is the common one – though perhaps more efficient, usually more effective, and certainly more visible. Few countries other than Japan show how effectively a natural instinct may be turned into a well-run business.

Japan's sex industry has been estimated as a ¥4 trillion ($40 billion) business. Just how this figure was arrived at and how it compares with those of other countries is not apparent, but it is very large – indeed, it is almost equivalent to the national defence budget.

And one fourth of this amount, also a very large sum, is from the revenue of the so-called love-hotels. Here is a venue which has effectively sustained and, to an extent, created Japan's sex bazaar. For while all societies have commercialized sex itself, only a few have marketed the place where it occurs, and none to the extent that Japan has.

There are over 35,000 such hotels, 3,000 in Tokyo alone. The rooms range in price from $40 to $100. This is for what is called in the parlance of the trade a 'short time'. A longer time, such as all night, costs more. Here the price climbs to the height of a certain all-night suite for $2,000, where – to be sure – you are allowed to occupy what is billed as a $10 million 'rococo' bed.

Prices differ for services offered. There are beds that rotate, or go up and down; mirror-lined rooms; two-level suites with a glass-bottomed bathtub intended to be viewed from below; a 'space-shuttle' bed for simulated take-offs and, for the ultimate in safe sex, an S/M chamber.

In addition many hotels serve breakfast, often including that popular 'stamina' food, broiled eel, and most rooms contain what is called a Romance Box, which contains whiskey, soap and a vibrator.

There is also the latest in TV electronics. Each room has a tube with closed-circuit pornography, and, many have self-operated cameras which relay the performance onto the tube – and, it is said, into the main office as well, where a further profit might then be made.

With such a variety of attractions it is not surprising that love-hotels out-rival Disneyland in popularity. The main reason for this acceptance, however, is the lack of venues anywhere else. Japanese dwellings are crowded and couples are correspondingly cramped, often having little choice other than these hotels.

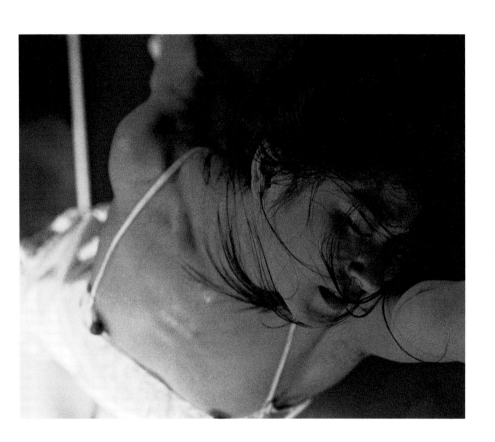

Consequently an amount of discretion is observed. The patrons often choose their room from an electronic menu, pressing the button for the desired chamber. The key is given them through a small window – that through which, at the end, they will pay the fee – and neither guest nor host is visible to one other (unless, of course, the former decides to take advantage of the TV camera in the room).

Since it has been ascertained through careful appraisal of the market that it is women who often choose which hotel to go to, the image itself has been sent up-market. Indeed the term 'love-hotel' is no longer much heard. Rather, one speaks of the 'fashion-hotel' or the 'leisure-hotel' and, while love-hotels have long had such names as 'Empire' and 'Rex', names with masculine associations, the fashion-hotels have names such as 'Chez Nous', the 'Inn Lively' chain, and the popular 'Once More'.

Although the Japanese businessman is often accused of rigidity (not adapting to circumstances, not accommodating, not opening up markets and so on), we can also see just the opposite, particularly if we compare the sex industry as it is now with what it was fifty years ago. Though pre-war Japan had a number of developed enterprises – quarters of prostitution in all the major cities, including the Yoshiwara in Tokyo and Shimabara in Kyoto – much was lacking on a less institutional level. Alternatives included venues with rooms by the hour where you brought a partner you yourself had already acquired – the *tsurekomi ryokan*, or 'drag them in inns'. Although there was as yet no law against prostitution (this was not instituted until 1957), there was also no alternative to quarters that marketed it, no room for free enterprise.

Likewise there was no catering to niche markets such as that which so distinguishes the contemporary sex market. There had

long been *kagema chaya*, 'boy teahouses', where men could meet, places proverbially patronized by the clergy, but there were no institutionalized locations where women could meet women. And any of the other minority tastes now so lavishly accommodated (fetishism, S/M, etc.) were ignored and business opportunities overlooked.

After the war, however, individualistic enterprise was encouraged, and markets were adjusted and expanded. The love-bathhouse is an example of such an adaptation. There had earlier been many such establishments but a nineteenth-century law closed their doors. When they reopened, it was necessary to assume a foreign guise.

Then, in 1984, a problem appeared. A Turkish diplomat complained that these baths – which had become the principal purveyor of the commodity after the passing of the post-war anti-prostitution laws – were called Turkish. Indeed *turuko* had become the most common term of referral.

The Tokyo-to Tokushu Yokujo Kyokai (Tokyo Special Bathhouses Association) met and eventually it was decided that the 110 affiliated bathhouses would change their designation. But to what? In order to determine this, the public, when appealed to, responded with numerous suggestions – more than two thousand of them. Among these contenders were Romanburo, Colt (that is, Koruto, a backwards rendering of Toruko) and Rabuyu (a felicitous combination of 'love bath' and 'love you') but the winner, hands down, was Sopurando, or Soapland.

Note the simplicity of the construction: a suggestion of cleanliness (soap), and a proposal of pleasure (Disneyland). This construction was an instant success, and prices then rose to match the level of dignity of the new title and more efficient money-making methods were employed.

Calling out a former attendant by name now costs a bit more; there appeared the unexplained but dignified *atobarai*, unspecified charges when you checked out; and the categories of service, special service, double service, extra special service, and full course (the last being what we might call making love) were more strictly insisted upon. But there were perks as well, for example the new 'fashion massage', a service which formerly the patron had perhaps practiced upon himself.

Another quarter of the sex market is concerned with the speciality venues. Here progress varies, but examples of enterprise include *kyabakura*, or cabaret clubs, which specialize in the somewhat uncomfortable but certainly stimulating activity called 'lap dancing'. There are *esthe* clubs, named after a famous beauty product, where 'sex massage', so billed, is available. And a recent venue is the *imekura* or 'image club' where special environments are available. There are mock nursery schools with girls in nurses' uniforms for men who wish to play baby; there are classrooms with girls in schoolgirl uniforms and the customer gets the blackboard and the chalk; there is the scaled-down railway car which involves molesting female strangers on the train, and which, in addition, offers part-time work to those employed underneath it providing the rocking motion so necessary to what is called a full image.

At the same time, some of the older venues are changing, for example that one-time favourite, the *nozoki-beya*. This, as the name indicates, is a small establishment where the clientele looks through peepholes at the main attraction (usually billed as a 'school-girl') performing within. The equivalent of a $10 bill is inserted to open the small hole and – at the more enterprising establishments – another bill opens a hand-sized window somewhat below waist level. These have been steady sellers for years, voyeurism having been heavily marketed in movies and *manga* alike. But the market had stabilized itself and even shown signs of falling off. Particularly, the charms of that lower window were found to be limited.

As though in answer, an innovation – from one of the workers herself – recently sprang into view. A customer had put in his customary bill and, instead of the window, the door opened. There, before the surprised patron, stood the girl herself. 'But you are supposed to be inside', he is quoted as having said. 'It's just too much trouble', said she as she pulled him to her.

Thus do institutions change their shapes and what is voyeurism's loss is business's gain. She pulled her patron into the much more lucrative mainstream and her independent action might be seen as just what the entrepreneur is capable of in a growth industry.

It is indicative that in this case the innovator was a woman because it has become increasingly evident that the female market is clamouring for attention. With the largest disposable income now in the handbags of unmarried women, the Japanese sex business is being transformed from a females-for-males service industry into a more level playing field.

The hostess club has long been an institution, but its opposite, the proliferating and highly lucrative host club, is relatively new. Here the female patron (just like her male counterpart) is surrounded by a highly attentive staff. Some host clubs have more than thirty hosts on their roster and all attempt to ingratiate themselves with the customers.

They dance, they light cigarettes, they offer towels, they laugh a lot and are good conversationalists, or at least attempt to be.

Though (like hostesses) they do not offer other talents outright, it is understood that these too are available.

Naturally, for a price – in this case a high one. On her first visit a client is charged only a relatively low first-time fee, say the equivalent of $100, and she must choose her main 'host' for future visits. He will then receive an up-front commission and half the take from her bills on her future visits. Hence perhaps all the ingratiating charm which surrounds the patron from the moment she opens the door.

Though a popular host scores dozens of clients he must be available to them all, must somehow remember their names, preferences, quirks, and at the same time spur each on to spend more money – imported brandy, hothouse fruit, etc., all at inflated prices. It is said that a full evening at a host club can be as expensive as $10,000. All of this without sex – so one may imagine what this must cost. Nonetheless, some 80 per cent of the hosts, it is said, sleep with their clientele.

Not many of the hosts allow themselves to be paid – that would run foul of Japan's disregarded but ever-present anti-prostitution laws. Instead the hosts graciously accept Hermes watches or Versace suits. Given the amount of money spent it is not surprising that several of the top hosts can gross, it is said, $8 million a year.

One is quoted (by Sayaka Yakushiji) as saying: 'I have nothing to feel ashamed about . . . Is it any different from being, say, a beautifican?' And another is quoted (by Lisa Cullen) as saying: 'Disneyland is a franchise that's attained global success by knowing what a child wants. If I can get women to love me as much as children love Mickey Mouse – and I can teach you how – is there any business that won't find value in that?'

There is another reason (besides 'love') for the new popularity of the host bar. Just as hostess clubs became socially acceptable only because they were necessary to the business culture, providing executives with a venue in which to soften up the clients, so, with more and more women climbing the business ladder, host bars are becoming respectable. They are losing their reputation of being sordid dens of gigolos. Rather, they are creditable. If the social acceptance of the hostess club indicated a male-dominated society, so the new status of the host bar reflects the coming claims of females. In any event, it is providing job opportunities for young males. At just one of the clubs more than thirty young men turn up every week to be interviewed.

Otherwise, however, finding enough personnel to staff the enormous sex industry in Japan is a problem. Men may be willing enough but finding women to work is a problem. A common ploy has been advertising. One publication, *Maru-Maru*, has hundreds of pages listing openings in clubs and the like, but most women remain leery. Recently, however, another means has been employed which is much more successful.

Young men roam the streets stopping young women. These males have been designed to approximate a type thought to be popular with young females – artificial tans, streaked hair, designer suits. They congregate in Shibuya or Shinjuku, Harajuku or Aoyama, and strike up conversations. Their object is to get the girl to agree.

If she agrees to visit a club, he will get $50, if she agrees to work there, $100. If the streaked-haired young man can talk ten girls into jobs he will, obviously, get $1000 – not at all bad for a day's work. This makes their methods exploitative but not all the women agree that they are exploited.

One of them, as quoted by Howard French, said that 'girls accept this kind of work all by themselves. I don't think people are dragged into it.' As for the work itself, another, a 23-year-old who said she had sex with three or four customers a day, stated: 'Sure it can be disgusting. But once you're in the business, the only hope is to save money for your future. Otherwise you've wasted your life.'

Not all is so up-market, however. Even within the speciality venues it would not do to paint too bright a picture. Though the various S/M establishments around town have shown a healthy gain, other markets have not; particularly disappointing has been that sober venue so misleadingly called the 'gay' scene.

Here it is a matter of mercantile concern that little development is occurring. Rising profit remains basic to any drinking establishment yet most of the male homosexual bars have, scandalously, not raised their prices in the last five years. Drinks, unbelievably in modern Japan, still cost a mere $7 and one is allowed, unaccountably, to nurse this single drink most of the evening. A note of hope, however, is that the female homosexual bars are among the most expensive in the city and snacks are served whether wanted or not – a sign that a sane business sense is prevailing.

In general, however, the so-called gay scene exhibits little economic promise. There are no racks of theme T-shirts, no guided tours, no Gayland concept at all. One interested store owner is quoted: 'If ever an area needed development it is this one.'

Leaving this depressing subject, it is a pleasure to turn to more forward-looking developments. One of the latest to hit the scene took advantage of the new technology in a highly dramatic form. There are still some bugs in the system but the signs are all there.

There opened in Tokyo's Shinjuku, the 'Kabuki-cho Virtual-Sex Salon'. While it did not last long enough to catch on with the general public, it was nonetheless written up in the popular press, although in such terms that it is difficult to ascertain precisely of what it consisted.

Apparently in addition to the helmet and glove of the more conventional virtual-reality wear, there was a digitalized codpiece. Though this itself contained a design flaw, depriving the franchise holder of the lucrative female market, the other defects in the apparatus were such that this small miscalculation went unremarked.

What occurred has been subject to some speculation but there was an apparent electrical failure. One young patron experienced, in the words of the reporting daily, a *gyaku funsha koka* – literally, a 'reverse jet-fountain effect'. Though otherwise uninjured, the patron refused a free trial run to take the place of the aborted experience and this led eventually to an official inquiry and the closure of the Kabuki-cho Virtual-Sex Salon, an establishment which had, after all, billed itself as 'The Ultimate in Safe Sex'.

But bugs in systems eventually get ironed out and where there is hardware, software will follow. It would be unwise to dismiss virtual sex as just a bad idea – rather one should think of it as a bad idea whose time has not yet come.

In contrast to such setbacks there are new and successful developments. One of the most innovative, and one which may be said to have milked its initial idea to the full potential, is the video box.

Like all great business concepts, the idea is simplicity itself: a large room in which stands a number of large boxes; the customer enters one of them and locks the door; this activates the TV into which he inserts his thousand yen bill; the soft-core porno

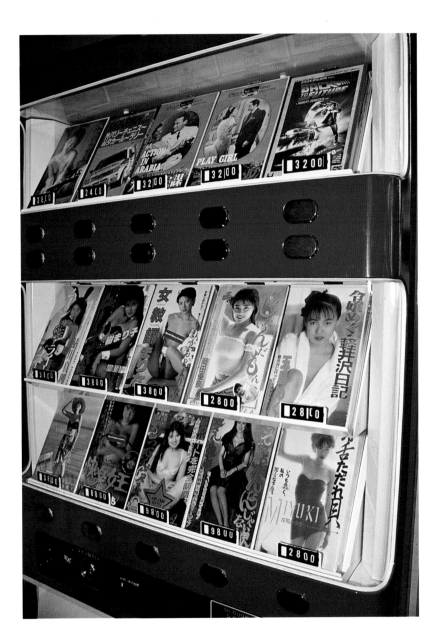

film begins. The only other accoutrements in the box are an open box of tissues and a waste-paper basket.

The clarity of the idea becomes apparent. Japanese business know-how, by harnessing one of nature's most universal urges, has persuaded the patron to pay for a pleasure hitherto wastefully free. One admires the sheer imagination necessary to take such successful advantage of such an enormous market.

Finally, new means of marketing too offer insights into the enterprising world of sex business in Japan. Here one of the most successful has been the vending machine. Not only do these purvey alcohol, tobacco, soft drinks and hot lunches, they now do their bit to satisfy an increasingly open demand.

There is, for example, the lucrative condom industry, big business indeed in this age of AIDS. Though for the up-market buyer there are now rubber boutiques, such as the extremely successful Condomania in that heartland of the young, Harajuku, there is no doubt that the greatest number of prophylactics are sold by the privacy-ensuring coin-operated machines.

In a bold new step these same machines are now also vending porn-video. No longer need the patron make the sometimes embarrassing visit to his corner shop. He (or she) can, in perfect anonymity, purchase porn for as little as $20 per title. This is to be certain the pornography called soft-core. To obtain what is known as hard-core, the corner shop must still be visited a number of times until mutual trust between owner and patron is built to the point where the area under the shelf is displayed.

The problem is that, since Japan has no censorship laws as such, there is a difficulty when it comes to defining what is obscene and what is not. For a time, a useful line was drawn at pubic hair. Anything with it was obscene, anything without it was not. This led to a number of anomalies, shaved models among them, but at least it defined the field. Magazines and books entering the country were routinely cleaned of hirsute details by squads of housewives working part-time and equipped with special equipment that scraped the areas free of any image whatsoever.

Now, the pubic-hair line is not holding. Magazines, even newspapers, breach it daily. To be sure, imported publications remain censored. *Playboy*, *Hustler* and the others are thoroughly scrubbed before going on sale, In Japanese publications, however, full frontal female nudity is allowed.

Not, however, male. Oshima Nagisa's film *In the Realm of the Senses* has never been shown uncut in Japan, and in its 'uncut' Tokyo revival in 2002 it remain censored. Now that the 'hair barrier' had been breached, it was no longer a social threat to show the actress whole, but whatever charms the actor possessed were still to be obscured by the digitalized lens. Such is the relative importance accorded men and women in this country.

As this indicates, a certain ingenuity is called for in marketing sex. Even so, some of the means are questioned. One such was the schoolgirl underwear vending machine. Its mercantile effectiveness is unquestioned: bought for as little as $1 per unit, the item was sold for as much as $50. In just a month the enterprising trio of men responsible made over $170,000. Obviously a public was out there; equally, there was an abundant source. The newly rich schoolgirls, working hard to use their underwear, playfully referred to their new employment as *H-baito*, the *baito* coming from *arubeit*, a common loan-word for part-time work, the *H* coming from the romanization of *hentai*, which means 'perverted'. Yet enterprise has its enemies. The Education Ministry took an interest and finally decided that these entrepreneurs may

have broken the Antique Dealings Act. The result was a closure of business.

One could go on and describe further the obstacles that have been put in the way of enterprise. For example, the necessary flyers for sexual services which so colourfully decorate so many phone boxes – brightly-coloured slips of paper which are removed by the authorities despite the cost. It was recently estimated that it cost Osaka ¥30 million in 1993 to clear away all the *pinku bira*, as these sticky bits of paper are called. But enterprise thrives on adversity. Resourceful business minds, put to work, have responded. Now NT&T has reported that sex service advertisements are being stamped in indelible ink on the telephone itself.

The future burgeons as more and more business outlets are being discovered. NT&T itself and the other communication giants might well avail themselves of the many sex-service lines, both professional and amateur, which now stretch across the country, catering to any appetite and creating not a few. Or the interested investor might consider stock in Gainex, a concern marketing explicit computer games. Although the current model features only a mild strip-tease, more, much more, is promised. And of course the new empire of the Internet offers not only porn for free but a gratis bulletin board for all sorts of romantic needs – some of them (though not yet enough) commercial.

These, then, are some examples of this highly successful commercialization of a commodity in Japan. Enterprise, imagination, application, and sheer single-mindedness have, in Japan, turned an instinct into an industry, have carved an empire from an urge.

Leisure Options

One of the indices of a culture is not only what it produces but how it relaxes. We are familiar with how hard Japan works, but perhaps have not yet heard of how hard Japan works to play. Yet these leisure choices contribute to the changing identity of the Japanese no less than do the various documents of fashion and fad.

This has long been true. Traditionally Japan divided its time into three separate categories. There was *ke*, which was normal work time. Then there was *kegare*, which was a kind of negative work, dealing as it did with the time taken up by activities such as birth and death; and in between, as it were, was *hare*, which was devoted to worship and such activities as festivals. The latter is near to what we would think of as leisure, even though the activity itself might be more demanding than work itself.

During a recession one might think people would be working ever harder, that there would be much more *ke* than *hare*, but this is not true. Japanese are at present working less and in this they are encouraged. Since sales are slow, production is not pressed. Companies that once demanded overtime now offer full vacations or early retirement. Before, you worked more for your country, now you work less for your country. And another incentive, of course, is that work is dangerous to health. There is death from overwork. Only Japan has a term for this peculiar sort of demise – *karaoshi* – but then only Japan has need for such a term.

What do you do when you yourself have to choose what to do? This was not encountered early because Japan is historically a poor country. Its wealth, in both money and time, and the visibility of the leisure choice are recent. So it is for most other countries as well, though perhaps not so dramatically, and we all react to new riches equally badly. Too, we predicate ourselves upon our work, and consequently wither when we retire; whether we are victims of the Protestant work-ethic or Japanese workaholism the result is the same. And the arising problems. What is interesting is the various ways in which we react and Japan's is one of the more varied.

The West is of several minds about work. The Bible would have us believe that leisure was paradise, for it was leisure that was lost when Adam and Eve had to go to work. Aristotle, however, believed that work meant being occupied by something desirable for its own sake, and this was the exercise of the speculative faculty, in its way a kind of leisure. Adam Smith, discounting leisure entirely, believed that it is through work alone that man comes to know himself, or at least his capabilities.

Japan would seem to parallel the Christian belief and its post-Reformation corollary that work is right, that it is the moral thing to do. It is upon this idea that the Japanese economy has long been posited. Leisure is thus equated with free time and this time is a negative quantity, since it is defined entirely as non-work. Free time leaves a work-orientated people at a loss.

In Japan the two-day weekend is still so new that, as a recent Postal Savings Promotion Society survey discovered, 75 per cent of those polled complained that these enforced holidays were both too expensive and too tiring. The expense was because most of the respondents spend the new hours either eating out or going shopping or both. The tiredness resulted from these activities and also from their having to think about how to fill the new time, also from the exhausting task of having to define through choice.

This is a problem. In Japan personal choice is usually obviated by group choice. When people go out to dine together, for example, they often all order the same thing. This demonstrates solidarity, always welcome in the country, and this obviates the difficulty of choice. To choose personally, however, is to experience, not freedom, but difficulty – as in the line at MacDonald's, where owing to the ordering system single choice is enforced, and long waits ensue as the person in front of you ponders at length.

Also, in Japan, leisure is usually supervised – as in Japanese schools, from kindergarten upwards, where play is always superintended. An unwelcome result of the *reja bumu* (leisure boom) was that there were not enough supervisors. People were left without a clue (not everyone obviously, but perhaps a majority) and the problem of what to do with free time looms large.

Confronted with this, the Japanese authorities studied leisure. The Prime Minister's Office found that on a given weekday 54.2 per cent of the populace spent its leisure time watching TV, listening to the radio, or reading newspapers and magazines. But, it further discovered, at the weekend these passive recreationists numbered only 31.6 per cent. What had happened? Perhaps they were out looking for leisure. This assumption fitted the findings of the Japan Leisure Development Centre (there is one), which found that only 37 per cent of the Japanese are satisfied with their leisure, as compared with the contented 80 per cent in Canada and Australia.

In that case they ought to be given an opportunity to be satisfied. Some sort of leisure facilities should be arranged. And if leisure could be marketed as well, then a profit might be made. The government itself could not take advantage of these findings but the business sector could. Large segments of the leisure market were already occupied by playing *pachinko* and reading *manga* 'comics' (avocations of which those polled perhaps did not inform the Prime Minister's Office), but there are others.

For example, *karaoke*. The term means 'empty orchestra', and the activity itself consisted originally of a mike and a pre-recorded musical background. Now, however, it included much else: TV-projected backdrop, Dolby effects, and other accoutrements. In Osaka where was a place with sprinklers and umbrellas which specialized in renditions of 'Singin' in the Rain', 'Stormy Weather', 'Raindrops Keep Falling on My Head', and other appropriate melodies.

The National Police Agency tells us that at their height there were 96,048 such venues and that *karaoke* ranked as the number one leisure pastime, slightly ahead of horse racing and *pachinko*. The average patron spent 2.2 hours singing 7.7 numbers, but the survey does not tell us whether this was weekly or daily.

Already *karaoke* was being widely exported. Korea was full of it, China as well. Even ex-President Clinton liked it. On a trip to Osaka he stayed out until two in the morning belting out songs with Yuya Satoshi, then president of Sanyo.

Karaoke, however, is not without its critics. Not on moral grounds, of course, but for reasons of noise pollution. It can usually be heard quite plainly outside the establishment in which it occurs. By law it must stop, in some neighbourhoods,

at midnight. There are ways around this, however. In Tokyo's Nihombashi an entrepreneur recently took to parking thirty *karaoke* vans in a vacant lot and letting rip.

Why the popularity? Various reasons are offered. The chance to be a safe 'star', safe in that everyone else gets to be a star too; the fact that we all like to sing, and that the latest in sound equipment makes us sound much better than we really are; and – a more likely reason – the group can be together and does not have to think of things to say. Indeed, talking is impossible since karaoke is so noisy. Moreover, it is a cheap way to use up leisure hours. Or it was during the bubble years.

Also in the *karaoke* machine we have yet another continuation of traditional Japanese culture. Noting that Japan has long had a tradition of entertainers whose sole purpose was to make the big spender feel okay about himself in the eyes of his peers, these practitioners have dubbed the *karaoke* machine the 'electric geisha'.

The recession, as well as the Walkman and the other portable devices, is now perhaps eroding the massive popularity of *karaoke*. A more real rival, however, is the portable telephone, the *keitai denwa*, which regularly breaks into one rendition after another and is besides a great time-taker in its own right, since it can now forward not only your phone call but also your e-mail, can connect you to the Internet, and may be programmed to contain a number of electronic games.

Much leisure is anodyne. *Manga* is important not for what it lets you see but what it keeps you from seeing – the other passengers in the train, for example. Walkman is a filter not for what you hear but for the city din that you do not. *Pachinko*, now a public institution, like a hospital, is an ideal way in which to spend leisure time – convalescing as it were. *Karaoke* idealizes a social situation. Not all leisure, however, is this passive – or, if so, is then passive in a different manner.

It has for some time been observed that foreign travel is one of the more popular ways of spending leisure time. It was also noticed that the foreign traveller is going further and further away. Originally it was Guam and Saipan, though now the only Japanese going there are new-rich farmers. Then it was Hawaii and Bangkok, places visited now by the lower urban middle-classes. The people with money go to London, Paris, Rome, or San Francisco, New York.

Travel within Japan – this is where profits have been found. Until the 1860s there was indeed no place else to go. Under the laws of seclusion citizens were not allowed out of the country and, if out, were not allowed back in. There was talk of execution as discouragement and perhaps a few Japanese were so dealt with. At the same time, there were certainly loopholes through which enterprising merchants or members of the military could slip out and in. Nonetheless, the mandate kept almost everyone else at home.

So there were no other sights to see except the local sites. Large fairgrounds supplied something for such early tourists to look at – the big site at the foot of the Ryogoku Bridge in Edo, for example. Here the onlookers could look at such educational exhibits as a large whale, a brace of dromedaries, an enormous image of Buddha made of oiled paper over basketry. There were also attractions which aimed only at entertainment. There was a giant toad made of velvet, there was the cannibal hag from Yotsuya, and the 'testicle girl', an unfortunate female who possessed a scrotum.

Also on view were some of the scientific wonders of the world, such as the telescope. Not that these were always used correctly.

Yajirobe, the hero of Jippensha Ikku's bestselling picaresque novel *Travels on Foot on the Tokaido* (Tokaidochu Hizakurige) puts one to his ear and can hear nothing.

He, along with his sidekick Kitahachi, takes us on one of the most popular excursions of the early nineteenth century, the pilgrimage to Ise. Though local travel was often discouraged by the authorities (there were barrier stations on all major roads, farmers were not usually allowed off their land, apprentices had only a few days off during the year), religious inclinations were respected, and a trip to the great religious centre of Shinto had to be encouraged.

The pilgrimage proved popular. As indeed it would in a country starved for diversion. Certainly a part of the intention was proper devotion, but around Ise there also grew an entire pleasure camp filled with all sorts of wonders and a number of pretty and compliant maidens as well. It was this aspect that Yajirobe and Kitahachi most looked forward to, the prostitutes of Ise having become one of the religious centre's most potent attractions.

Not nowadays, however. Ise is now unadorned, though there is a sanitized and gentrified 'theme park' there. Atami, home of the honeymooner and also a 'geisha' centre, has became an economic wasteland; other meccas for the newly spliced, traditionally sources of a sizeable income, such as Kyushu's Ibusuki Jungle Baths, eventually came to host only the relatively badly heeled honeymooners from Taipei and Seoul. True, with today's local economy it is cheaper for Japanese to go to Paris than to go to Okinawa, but even so there should be some way to get all of that leisure, otherwise wasted, to remain in Japan.

A kind of solution to this problem was found. Using the highly successful Disneyland as model, a large number of new theme parks opened. The themes were mainly foreign. As the travel writer Cleo Paskal has written, 'today's Japanese tourists don't want to be bothered by the horror, not to mention the expense and trouble, of the real thing. They want a New York they can visit for a weekend, and a London where everyone speaks Japanese. They want a sanitized, Japanese version of the rest of the world – a virtual vacation.' This virtuality is, of course, what Disneyland has so profitably dispensed. It is, indeed, the theme of one of its attractions: 'It's a Small World'.

Japan created a replica of Deshima, the seventeenth-century prison-home to the first foreigners, so it was here that modern Japanese could visit a part of their own culture. So popular was this venture that the parent company later opened up Huis Ten Bosche, an enormous area packed with canals, windmills, tulips, cheese and wooden shoes. There are 'European-style' hotels and those who wish could buy an on-site Dutch house right in the park and live the life of the Nederlands burger without ever having left Japan. Also there was, naturally, none of the dinge and danger of, say, Amsterdam. The original Dutchman could, from his island, view Japan as spectacle, now the Japanese can view Holland as spectacle, all from the comfort and safety of their own land. During its first year, Huis Ten Bosch had nearly four million well-paying customers. The popularity has since much lessened but at least the place is still open.

Not so, many of the others. Ashibetsu in Hokkaido – having lost its coal-mining industry – decided to go into the theme-park business and opened Canada World: Japan's largest lavender field, a complete Prince Edward Island-like, Anne of Green Gables Land, and seven resident Canadians quilting, playing the fiddle, chopping wood. This venture, one is sorry to say, did not last long enough to realize a profit.

In Niigata's Russian Village one could, without the difficulty and danger of actually visiting Russia, see the Cathedral of the

Birth of the Virgin at Suzdal, eat pirozhki and borsch, and enjoy a folk song and dance troupe and the talents of three performing seals direct from Lake Baikal. Over in Shingomura in Aomori one might also visit the last resting-place of Jesus Christ. It was actually his brother, Iskiri, who was crucified, you see. Christ himself escaped to Japan. He married a Shingomura woman named Yumiko, had three daughters, and lived to a happy 106 years of age. It is his 'descendants' who have opened up this Christ's Tomb tourist attraction.

Then there was Nixe Castle in Noboribetsu, a full-scale replica of the castle at Odense, Hans Christian Andersen's home-town; Shuzenji's Britain Land, a slice of seventeenth-century British countryside complete with homes and shops. In Kure there was Portopialand, which included much of Portugal's Costa do Sol in some form or other.

Plus a number of New-Zealand-Valleys in Hiroshima, Yamaguchi and Shikoku, several of which still specialize in sheep shows, an exotic entertainment in non-mutton-eating Japan, and, in addition, Yomiuri Land, the only recently closed Yokohama Wild Blue swim-drome, the Chiba Hawaiian Center (with wave machine), and – a sure winner – Hello Kitty Land.

Then, for those in a hurry, there is the Tobu World Square, where one may at leisure view 1/25 scale models of more than one hundred of the world's most famous buildings all at once. The Taj Mahal is next to the Empire State Building, which is next to St Peter's, which is next to the Eiffel Tower, and so on. All are complete down to the smallest visible detail (they were made by the Toho Eizo Bijutsu, the people who gave us *Godzilla*) and they offer the world at a glance.

Though the onlooker at these spectacles may be reminded of Dr Johnson's maxim that nothing is more hopeless than a

scheme of merriment, the financial success of at least some of these various artificial foreign lands within the safe confines of Japan has proved their local viability.

After all, places like Canadian World actually let one become a temporary Canadian, whereas if one visited Canada there is the constant reminder that one is actually a foreigner. And, in any event, foreign countries are just too foreign to be readily comprehensible. These 'translated' versions are, it is believed, the best way of understanding them.

This is a virtual world, superior in many ways to the virtual-reality machines where you have to wear outfits to get the illusion. Here the illusion is provided naturally and effortlessly and can be cut into any size to fit anyone's leisure. It is still subject, however, to the vagaries of the real world.

As Japan drifted off into recession and then depression one vibrant theme park after another closed. Although there were incentives to local travel (the destruction of the Trade Center towers and the resulting fear of air travel proved a true boon to local travel agents), getting the most out of the leisured Japanese tourist is still a problem.

These then are but some of the ways in which Japan spends its leisure time. They are not that much different from those of other countries, but there are enough differences to indicate that the new availability of leisure finds the Japanese unprepared and, more seriously, that new leisure undermines some of the ideas upon which Japanese traditional culture rested.

Traditionally, Japan learned to transform its poverty. The Japanese sense of space was determined by not having much furniture, the art of pottery is predicated upon having lots of mud, and not so much else. The art of the small, the minimal, the

enormous economy of spatial assumptions, this was due to not having much. Prime aesthetic values, such as those distinguished under such untranslatable terms as *sabi* and *wabi*, were based upon want.

After a thousand years or so of this, suddenly, about thirty years ago, Japan got rich – not the *Japanese,* of course, but Japanese institutions including its politicians. It is not surprising that the result was a pack of *nouveaux riches* large by any standards, a plethora of leisure and a new height of public vulgarity.

A result has been the trivialization of tradition. The tourist is invited to the old. A Japan Travel Board poster for such tours shows a modern young thing in jeans exclaiming in delighted shock at the sight of a thatched roof.

Since tradition now has few functions, it has been gentrified into a simulcrum of itself. In the newly redesigned Asakusa in old downtown Tokyo the real Edo period shrines now look the more plastic. The Disney-like hotchpotch of Edo-mura, a commercial reconstruction of parts of the old capital, can now be visited out in the rice-fields of Tochigi. To the attentive tourist it is apparent that Kyoto has become Kyoto Land. And all because of the splendours and miseries of tourism as a leisure activity.

A study of a people's leisure rarely results in a pleasing aesthetic view, to be sure, but in the case of Japan we have the added drama of a people trying to cope with the personal choice that leisure insists upon. Plato holds that democracies have a passion to spend rather than to save, to enjoy rather than to possess, to desire luxury rather than moderation. If this is true then leisure spending follows the commercial and democratic spirit. How Japan is spending its leisure time thus affords an index of its commercial and governmental identities. It also offers the always enlightening spectacle of a nation learning to create self through choice.

Manga Culture

The proliferation of *manga* comic-books in Japan and the attitudes and expectations they engender is well documented. Though this long-lasting fad is slowly passing, it has been not only of social but also of economic importance.

At its height, around 1995, the *manga* magazine industry yearly made more than the equivalent of two billion dollars, and the most popular were reprinted into books that made over one billion more. Shogakukan, the most influential *manga* publisher, issued twenty million copies a month. The most widely 'read' had a circulation of four million – a large number, about half the population of Osaka, Japan's second largest city.

These were seen by a large and increasingly adult population – about fifteen copies for every man, woman and child in Japan. A spokesman from Kodansha, another large publisher, said that 'it used to be that when students graduated from high school they also graduated from *manga*', but not now. It is reported that Hashimoto Ryutaro, when prime minister, used to spend a quiet evening at home looking at *manga* with his wife and until recently it was common to see adults on trains and subways reading little else.

Despite the fact that most Japanese *manga* are made up of violence and sex, there are actually funny comics as well. *Manga* arrived early in Japan. Caricatures and comic drawings have been found in the seventh-century Buddhist temple complex of Horyuji at Ikaruga, and in the eighth-century Toshodaiji at Nara. In the famous twelfth-century *Choju Jinbutsu Giga* scroll drawings of various birds and beasts satirized nobles and monks of the period.

In the Kamakura era (1185–1333) illustrated scrolls were depicting the Buddhist heaven and hell and comically recording the foibles of the day. In the later Edo period (1600–1868) new printmaking methods found a large audience for the graphic exaggerations of the *otsu-e* and the *toba-e*, leading to the comic portraits of Sharaku, Hokusai and, later, Kuniyoshi and Kobayashi Kiyochika. Also during the Taisho period (1912–26) the proliferation of magazines and newspapers made popular the work of such cartoonists as Okamoto Ippei, and later the work of Tezuka Osamu. It was the latter who is usually credited with creating the post-war *manga* form.

This he did by modelling his work on the multi-panelled comic strip, which had been introduced in the USA at the end of the nineteenth century. This was not the usual one- or two-panel comic or satirical cartoon with which Japan had been familiar, but a strip, a continuous story told like a movie in panels or scenes and approximating the storyboard, itself often used in the construction of films. Dialogue was shown in the American manner ballooning from the mouths of the characters rather then merely alongside them as in conventional Japanese prints and *e-maki* hand scrolls.

The imported storyboard-like format was thus in a way familiar and allowed a continuation of what might be considered a native narrative requirement, one identified by the *manga* scholar Natsume Fusanosuke as 'an emphasis on an interesting storyline and an ease of reading'. It also encouraged some innovations.

Tezuka Osamu is usually credited with bringing the visual conventions of film to *manga*, simulating the zooms and pans of the camera, as well as the long shots and the close-ups. In his 1947 *New Treasure Island* comic-book series, we see the hero driving his car, all shots 'taken' from multiple viewpoints covering a double page. This was at a time when Western comics were drawing static panels filled with dialogue balloons. He is also credited with the decidedly un-Japanese look of the cartoon character.

This, says Dave Kehr, was because – influenced by both Disney's early Mickey Mouse and Max Fleischer's Betty Boop, both of them newspaper cartoons, as well as animated short subjects – he imitated their 'simple, spherical construction', particularly in his popular *manga* of 1951, *Astro Boy*. The statue-like body of the creature (he was a robot) was topped by a noticeably large head, with unusually large round eyes. Though there are many reasons why popular Japanese cartoon characters do not look Japanese, one of them is that the 'father of *manga*' drew them that way.

As for action, both early and late *manga* follow traditional narrative. One might say that American comics resemble illustrated narratives but that Japanese comics resemble visualized narratives. *Manga* decompresses story lines. Instead of ten or twenty pages, the Japanese 'comic' book uses hundreds of pages. The result is far fewer words (indeed, the 'word' is used only for dialogue and for onomatopoeia) and something approximating a film.

A further reason for popularity is that the 'word' is not only de-emphasized but it is also simplified so that all *manga* 'read' like

children's books even if they are intended for adults. Someone once pointed out that Michelangelo painted the Bible for people who couldn't read. Perhaps such illiteracy is behind the popularity of the *manga* book. Though Japan likes to pride itself on having the highest literacy rate in the world, its standards for literacy are not those of other countries. Most high school graduates can read only several thousand *kanji* and cannot cope with an author, such as Mishima Yukio, who is fond of odd terms and difficult combinations.

For whatever reason then, *manga* remained a preferred form of narrative. In Japan even company newsletters came out in *manga* form, there is a cartoon *Tale of Genji* and Akio Morita's *Made in Japan*, the Sony saga, appears as a comic.

The reader scans the image and receives an impression of plot and character, along with major assumptions about the nature of reality. A *manga* of some three hundred pages takes about twenty minutes to read. That means sixteen pages per minute or slightly less than four seconds per page. Like a portable but leisurely TV set the image-propelled entertainment is perused in less than half an hour, then the *manga* is discarded (I have never heard of one being 'read' twice). Each costs the equivalent of about two dollars and, though the price is low by Japanese standards, the profit for the publishers is considerable.

As for the content, Frederick Schodt, the Western authority on the subject, has said that '*manga* are the direct descendants of popular art . . . in the late Edo period (1600–1867), art in which exaggerated sexuality and stylized violence – scenes of samurai disembowelling themselves and bloodspatters – were a standard feature.'

He also says that 'even if they are basically trash . . . they are harmless entertainment', implying that they are no direct

reflection of Japanese society. It is difficult, however, not to see some representation when *manga* not only reflects the values of Japanese society but, to an extent, creates them – though not to the extent of another image-powered entertainment, that great social builder, television.

Both, however, represent an alternate way of 'reading', one which most resembles scanning or the 'fast reading' techniques of the West. Speed is, if not the aim, then the result and comprehension is confined to the surface. Since little appeal other than recognition is demanded, little effort is required in looking at *manga* or in regarding the tube. The simplified version of reality that results is consequently rarely disturbing and this in part might account for the popularity.

Though *manga*-mags are now less popular (now that people have cell phones to keep hands, eyes and ears busy), their influence is no less prominent. What we might call *manga*-mode is everywhere. It is a favourite advertising style, it influences all forms of graphics from book design to cinematic composition, it has created the very look of the Net and the Web.

Turn on and you are confronted with various cute creatures selling things, little pop-up surprises in the form of cartoon characters. These are presented in boxes or containers or within borders which one recognizes from the *manga* page. And the Internet or Website narrative moves according to *manga*-mode as well.

In Japan, perhaps more than in most countries, the appeal of *manga*-mode is near universal and consequently no other form of narrative has been followed so widely. The simple sequential is all that is demanded – if effect follows cause, that is enough. The primitive *manga* narrative consequently becomes the single chronology that is most widely used. In advertisements, in most

new films, in novels such as those by Yoshimoto Banana, *manga*-like structure becomes the preferred narrative.

Manga magazines themselves appear complicated when compared to the simplicities of the game programs and the elemental possibilities of the cell phone through which they are increasingly played. The tiny screen can contain only a certain amount of information. E-mail can barely manage the means of narrative. Icons can barely (smiling face/frowning face) suggest the emotions one is supposed to feel.

At the same time, however, *manga*-mode can be personalized in a way that *manga*-mags cannot. Just as game fantasies can be tailored to the user's needs, so the cell phone screen can be set to answer expectations. Perhaps *manga*-mags are no long so popular because they are too explicit, they allow no room for the viewer. Cell phone entertainment, however, does.

Hence, eyes that were once glued to the page are now pasted to the palm of the hand. One might argue that cell phone (and electronic Game Boy) fantasies at least allow a kind of choice which the predetermined *manga* does not, but one may do so only if one believes that such a severely limited range of options amounts to a choice.

The attractions of this simplicity are manifest, however. It has made Japan a much less complicated land, a much easier place in which to live, and also the one, in many ways, now least in touch with the unfortunate verities of human existence.

Pachinko

If a fad is what is created by a large number of enthusiasts, then *pachinko* is the biggest fad of them all – more than twenty million devotees daily. Yet while other Japanese fads – *karaoke*, Hello Kitty, Pokemon – are already well known elsewhere, *pachinko* has so far resisted exportation.

Perhaps this is because of its radical differences from its nearest Western relative, pinball. Unlike this restful, nearly horizontal game, *pachinko* is aggressively vertical, taller than the player, and noisy. While pinball indicates the score with a few flashing lights and a couple of bells, the sound of the moving balls itself softened with padded obstacles and rubbered baffles, *pachinko* was designed to be bright and loud.

The name itself expresses the din. It is an onomatopoeic term imitative of the noisily racketing ball (*pachin*) and the clack it makes when it hits its targets (*ko*). The won balls swirl into the metal tray at the bottom with the roar of a molten torrent, while over it all bellows a full-volume sound system.

This cacophony is nationwide. There are three million machines in sixteen thousand halls serving one quarter of the whole population, sitting there and contributing what is estimated at $300 billion – much more than the defence budget, even more than the gross national product of Switzerland.

The colossal fad of *pachinko* is a post-war phenomenon. Though a primitive form (based on the American pinball-like Corinthian Game) was known in Japan as early as the 1930s, *pachinko* itself did not evolve until the war was lost. In those hardship times there was little amusement and certainly few other ways to win some of the candy and cigarettes that were given out as prizes.

As the market developed so did the machines, the policies of the venues and the techniques of the management. From simple stalls the *pachinko* parlours grew into the mighty palaces which now stud landscapes both urban and rural. From an affair with a spring-handle and nails about which coursed the balls, the machine itself became computerized and developed an electronic spin-handle, then digital electronics were incorporated, an embedded TV tube added the attractions of the slot machine, the resulting hybrid being called the *pachisuro*.

This emphasized the gambling potential that has always been behind *pachinko's* popularity, getting something for nothing being everywhere everyone's desire. Hence equally streamlined became the methods of pay off. Originally winners received soap, towels, toilet paper, which could be sold to affiliated outlets somewhere at the back of the *pachinko* parlour. Shortly, however, *pachinko* balls were being exchanged for tokens (*bunchin*) and these were taken to small cash stalls (*kaiba*, more properly *keihin kokanjo*, prize-exchange facilities) in the vicinity where they were exchanged for money.

The reason for this separation of game from pay-off is that *pachinko* as overt gambling would break several laws. Covert gambling, however, can circumvent local jurisdiction. In Japan a physical separation, usually a matter of a half-minute stroll, satisfies the authorities. There is also a like division of apparent ownership. The *pachinko* halls are licensed as entertainment and usually run chain-store style. (It is said that the owners are usually Koreans and that *pachinko* might be called an act of revenge for the long and calamitous Japanese occupation of the Korean peninsula.) The money stalls, however, are rumoured to be run by the *yakuza*, that Mafia-like network of guilds which in Japan controls gambling as well as drugs, prostitution, extortion and similar money-making institutions.

It is said that the yakuza connection is also responsible for the recent image changes of both the halls themselves and the way they are managed. Originally *pachinko* was to be found only in lower-class entertainment districts, the *sakariba*. The custom was raffish and much of the noise was that of the wartime 'Gunkan March'. Such music also comprises the favourite melodies of the right-wing soundtracks which continue deafeningly to parade the streets of the major cities. Though the connections between yakuza and the right wing (and the construction industry, and the Japanese government) remain indubitable, any attempt at respectability would have to make these connections less visible.

Some reform has been adopted, however unsuccessfully. At one point it was thought that a larger potential female market (a quarter of the patrons are women) could be created if a more pastel and less deafening environment were offered – decor lavender and pink, Percy Faith on the sound system. Large sums were spent but patrons stayed away, women included. Thus, despite the many women playing *pachinko*, the atmosphere is still perceived as resolutely masculine – elemental colours and deafening noise.

This cacophony is apparently necessary. Consequently the contemporary *pachinko* parlour has improved it. Now techno-rock of various stripes is blasted out and above it are the shouted exhortations of hired men and women who, in the manner of unusually noisy disc jockeys, add to the racket which is so much a part of the game.

In this aural inferno sit long lines of patrons, each before his or her machine, oblivious of his or her neighbour. He or she is usually smoking and so the pollution of the air matches that of the ears. It brings to mind the worst of the nineteenth-century factories, humans themselves half-machine, the assembly line gone mad. At the same time, looking at the busy hands, the empty eyes, one also thinks of some kind of religious ceremony, something vaguely Tibetan with mandalas visible and prayer wheels whirling.

Yet these people seem to be enjoying themselves. They have paid for the privilege of sitting there and twirling their electronic spin-handles. Many stay for hours, intent, immune alike to discomfort and to din. Punishment, revelation – the inner joys of *pachinko* lie somewhere between the two.

While the participants think of it as merely a form of compensated leisure, *pachinko* has also been called (by Wolfram Manzenreiter) a diversion which emphasizes 'the commercialized, industrialized, and bureaucratized character of play behavior in a mass society'.

If play it is, then *pachinko* has been constituted into its most efficient form. In the West, the charm of pinball is often wastefully social. A number of people lounge around the machine.

Body English is observed and encouraged, monosyllables are exchanged. The machine itself may be struck or otherwise encouraged. Light refreshments are often nearby and an atmosphere of relaxed play is achieved.

Also, though the single individual pitted against a machine may be observed, more usually a loose group is involved. And, in any event, the pinball hall has other attractions – the bar, the many different kinds of play-machines, attractive strangers. The ambience is relaxed, friendly and sociable.

How different the *pachinko* hall. It contains nothing but row after row of machines. There is otherwise only the hand-basin, the toilet, the overflowing ashtrays. There are no amenities, only necessities. Nor does one eat or drink, or (because of the racket) talk. There is no soft lighting, only overhead glare. No innocuous mood music, only the steady beat of designer rock and the urgent and earnest shouting of the *pachinko* deejays. And there are few attractive strangers. Fellow players never hold conversations, much less encourage anything more.

Here sit the millions, each one sober in front of the machine, intent, earnest, feeding in the silver balls. There is no form of communication. There is not even Body English (or Japanese), since the machines cannot be maltreated. They are our equals, not our servants. Serious, even dedicated, each person sits before his moving mandala. If it were not for the noise one might think of a church, so personal is each person's activity.

Row upon row the faithful sit, as though in confessional booths. The ambience is closed, solitary. *Pachinko* is an intensely private occupation. There is nothing sociable about it. Yet, side by side, elbow by elbow, these people are, one might think, nevertheless in a kind of social situation. Perhaps, but there is no talk, no meeting of eyes, each sitting solitary, each communicating solely with a demanding machine.

Of what is one reminded in this monumental display of play? Why, of course, of work. One Japanese critic, Tada Michitaro, has argued that the relation between man and machine not only determines work processes but extends into the private sphere, that *pachinko* is thus not a pastime but a preparation for and a continuation of occupational education. Other critics, particularly those writing for the official *pachinko* journal (there is one), speak encouragingly of the individuality within the group, maintaining that they see the diversion as nurturing and explaining the brightness and the loudness as necessary playtime indicators.

Other scholars have mentioned that the pattern of work determines the pattern of leisure, and that self-fulfilling leisure is necessary as relief from alienating work. Both assumptions seem in this case true and one may agree with Manzenreiter that, here, genuinely Japanese qualities are matched by a genuinely Japanese game.

Perhaps this then is the reason that *pachinko* has not been exported from Japan. A concession did open in Germany but was shortly found financially wanting. This, however, has not kept other foreign buyers from displaying interest. A British firm, the BS Group PLC, explored possibilities with a Japanese group, the Tokyo Plaza Co., owned by the Korean-born Suh Dong Ho, whose company controls some seventeen gaming centres, making him Japan's fifteenth largest *pachinko* operator.

As the BS Group's chief executive officer, Clarke Osborne (quoted by Will Hollingworth), said: 'Success is measured by how people repeat their playing. *Pachinko* has colour, noise and speed, and these three elements combine to make this to the player very attractive.'

However, he added, negotiations were moving slowly. As indeed they would be. *Pachinko* addiction was created in Japan by a number of specific conditions and it is unlikely that Europe could recreate all of them. Let us consider a few of these.

In Japan the true purpose of the player would seem to have little to do with the ostensible aim of his efforts. If we take his winnings to be his wages then he is vastly underpaid for the amount of man-hours he puts in. Perhaps that is the reason that a publication called *The Pachinko Winners' Guide* is so popular. It still sells 400,000 copies bi-monthly, and David Plotz has noted the number of articles on 'pachinko bankruptcy' – noting that the biggest advertisers in the publication are consumer credit companies.

What the player normally takes home after a hard day in the *pachinko* palace averages out at much less than that allowed by the minimum wage law. If it were not, the *pachinko* business itself would not be making the amounts of money that it does.

In addition, whatever laws govern luck are openly disregarded. Every player knows that the machines are fixed. Either the nails in the old models were nightly bent by the proprietor (or his spin doctor) or in the new models the appropriate electronic fine-tuning is accomplished. Eric Prideaux quotes one owner: 'If my customers never win, they'll have no reason to come back. If they win too much I get crunched. It's about finding the proper balance. The hardest part is making the nails look lucky when really they're not.'

Gambling is, to be sure, addictive. One either plays *pachinko* a lot or one plays it rarely, if at all. We thus go to *pachinko* as we go to the bottle. That the millions thus addicted give rise to no national concern would indicate that the effects are found either benign or necessary.

Law enforcement agencies would find them both. And here they are following what might be identified as a national pattern. The ideologies of Japan encourage a portion of the public to gamble, fostering a dependency no less real than that upon alcohol, tobacco and other drugs. Indeed Japan has unusually strong lobbies to protect profits thus engendered. In their success they employ an agenda of social control – that which so distinguished the country in its early history and has continued healthy to the present day.

At the same time, although the *bakufu* government of the pre-modern Tokugawa period might (and has been) described as totalitarian in its methods, it rarely encroached into the further recesses of private life. Sexuality was never moderated so long as it did not disturb an appearance of social respectability. Likewise gambling. Only when there are public complaints do the Japanese forces of order move.

One might say that gambling, like sexual expression and much else, is encouraged in that such activities provide a kind of relief from the pressure that is otherwise exerted, that *pachinko* and prostitution are just two of the valves which keep the Japanese pressure cooker from exploding. Gambling as addiction is thus, as it were, officially sponsored. But one must then ask: What is this addiction a palliative for?

When we think of images for Japan, among the first to occur are no longer Mt Fuji or cherry blossom, but rather the *karaoke* room and the *pachinko* parlour, those entertainments that one sociologist, Ishige Naomichi, has said seem somehow to have been 'designed specifically for the Japanese mentality'. Here one may ask why anyone would become habituated to sitting in the cold or the heat, assailed by noise, with no hope of a reward commensurate to that paid for any other kind of work. For reasons we must turn again to the origins of the game.

Pachinko sprang directly from defeat. Even before the ruined cities were fully reconstructed, *pachinko* parlours had sprung up. The press referred to them as inexpensive places of pleasure in an otherwise pleasureless and poverty-stricken land. And even today there is an air of the immediate post-war era about these venues – the spartan if tawdry interiors, the bare necessities and nothing more, the long grey lines of patrons every morning waiting for the *pachinko* parlour to open. It was here that the thousands sought and found.

In Kurosawa Akira's film *Ikiru*, released in the autumn of 1952, merely seven years after the end of the Second World War and only a year after the end of the Occupation of Japan, the doomed hero, soon to be dead, is led into a *pachinko* hall and told: 'See this little silver ball? That is you, that's your life. Oh, this is a marvellous machine, a marvellous machine that frees you from all of life's worries . . .'.

It was not pleasure that was found, but oblivion. And this rewarded search has continued because the conditions that created it have continued. In the decades following the war Japan has vastly improved in all ways but one. No substitute has ever been discovered for the certainty that this people enjoyed until the summer of 1945.

A tightly knit population, an enormous single family, Japan suffered a trauma that might be compared to that of the individual believer who suddenly finds himself an atheist. Japan lost its god, and the hole left by a vanished deity remains. The loss was not the emperor, a deity suddenly lost through his precipitate humanization. It was, however, everything for which he and his whole ordered, pre-war empire had stood. It was certainty itself that was lost. And this is something that the new post-war world could not replace.

Indeed, the social fabric was even further rent. The individual, never allowed or later taught any individual reliance, was eventually deprived of any real emotional kinship with country, with town or city, and finally with family. And all of this occurred in only five decades.

The various pressures of city life are consequently felt strongly in Japan, and *pachinko* is a big-city phenomenon, even now that every country crossroads has its parlour. *Pachinko* first appeared in the greyest of the industrial cities, Nagoya and Osaka. Alhough originally the patrons may have been the jobless and the hopeless, now it is those for whom the job is not enough. These repair to the *pachinko* parlour as do others to further areas of addiction – bars, for example.

Like people in bars, those in the *pachinko* halls feel no pain. Instead, it might be argued, they are experiencing a sort of bliss. This is because they are in the pleasant state of being occupied, with none of the consequences of thinking about what they are doing or considering what any of it means. They have learned the art of turning off.

In this attainment boredom is a requisite. Yet some kind of activity – the droning of prayers or the monotone of machines, the telling of the beads or the clicking of the balls – is also necessary. The ritual may seem empty but it is not. It is filled with nothing. Oblivion is achieved.

Pachinko is thus, like all important distractions, only ostensibly about itself. Its true aim is far greater, this being nothing other than annihilation. The annihilation of self leads to a pleasant state, and may – for those successful – be prolonged indefinitely. The wordless communication between man and machine is just enough to offer an edge of oblivion, to keep the patron partially conscious of what he is doing, to keep him aware of his ostensible purpose in being there, while, at the same time, gratefully surrendering his real reason. The *pachinko* palace patron emerges refreshed, renewed.

One is reminded again of a religious exercise because the *pachinko* hall is, in its way, a kind of shrine, a sort of temple. One is reminded of *zazen* meditation, one of the aims of which is liberation from the self through the stilling of that very self.

When one meditates one does not think. Expressly, the aim of meditation is to prevent the normal grazing pattern of the unleashed mind. In meditation one is expected to curb the activities of this organ, which is solely responsible for any idea of self at all.

An aid to this is the ambiguous. The *roshi* may give the adept a seemingly meaningless riddle, a *koan,* to turn over and over in his head. This keeps the brain busy but prevents it from once more wandering the rut-like patterns which it has established and calls the self. Any answer to the riddle is arbitrary, but this arbitrary quality is not even recognizable until a degree of liberation from the mind and its ways has been achieved.

The *pachinko* machine may thus be seen as just such an arbitrary object. One does not in any true sense win with it. Rather, it occupies the attention and hence the mind. Both eyes and brain fastened to its shiny, noisy surface, the intelligence is blessedly stilled. The enigmatic mechanical face merges with one's own. Lulled by the racket, fascinated by the glare, you are alone, a community of singularity, and the familiar and contradictory self is allowed to rest.

Pachinko in this way resembles not only drink, but also drugs, sex, fast driving, religion. It affords relief from self, now that this self – constricted, conscribed, yet denied both security and certainty – turns upon itself to create the state we call alienation. No wonder *pachinko* is habit-forming. It is respite.

That it is nothing more remains its limitation. *Zazen* begins only after the mind is properly stilled. *Pachinko* does nothing more after this stillness is accomplished. *Zazen* is a true medicine. *Pachinko* is only a palliative.

Still, whether *pachinko* palace or *pachinko* barracks, the game has become an institution – like the public hospital. *Pachinko* therapy offered at a modest price has, however, never been openly recognized. The game is officially thought a harmless pastime and is ignored if not encouraged. And if you ask a player why he is there he always says that he is killing time.

Actually, he is killing much more than that. He is smothering the importunate and dissatisfied self. This he is doing – and again a Buddhist parallel is discernible – by living the present moment, the instant now, his mind focused. He is calm, at rest, at peace. Cut off from the world by his magical machine, he regards the tide of the balls as saints are said to regard the ebb and flow of the world. The resulting illumination is not lasting but it is, as the continued and enormous popularity of *pachinko* indicates, better than none at all.

The Convenience Phone

There is no denying the convenience of the convenience phone. It has shrunk our world and had an enormous impact on our social life. At our fingertips is not only everyone from business contacts to loved ones, but also the wonders of e-mail, pop tunes, games galore, and just around the corner, TV images and the whole upside-down cornucopia of the internet itself. And all of this in the palm of the hand, a whole cosmos, like an orb in the fist of a lord.

We are familiar with the uses of this portable phone in emergencies, in business transactions, in social negotiations – these are worldwide but nowhere more evident than in Japan. Here too are those extra benefits, noted elsewhere as well but here dramatically enlarged.

Take for example the dramatic drop in smoking. This was first noticed in England where the anti-smoking group ASH (Action on Smoking and Health) issued a report. A spokesman said that 'there is an incredible overlap between what smoking and mobile phone use means to kids – membership of a peer group, something to do with their hands, something to be stylish and adult with and something to be a bit rebellious about.'

At the same time mobile phones are marketed in a similar way to cigarettes and their use is expensive enough that what used to be cigarette money is now used up by the phones. Though this is viewed as a good thing ('anything that might prevent teenagers getting hooked on this deadly habit has got to be encouraging news') there is at the same time the fact that teenagers (particularly in Japan) are getting equally hooked on the portable phone (*keitai denwa*) habit. In Japan then one habit has been traded for another.

And is it deadly? Some think so. Mark Scheiber, reporting on electromagnetic waves messing up the brain, added that 'judging from the hordes of cell-phone zombies on the streets, compelled to check their e-mail every thirty seconds, such critics may be right'.

And, aside from the unproved report that use may result in brain cancer, and a recent investigation where earthworms shrivelled up after too many calls, there is the accident rate. People deep in conversation while driving, while standing too close to the platform edge as the train pulls in – their stricken numbers reached such heights that, in Japan, a Road Traffic Law was put into effect in 1999 banning the use of mobile phones while driving. Such a law is not to be enforced, however , and teenagers are still visible talking into one hand while driving with the other.

On the other hand, there are reports of much quieter classrooms. Usually noisy and noticeably inattentive, Japanese students now sit silent at their desks, apparently paying the closest attention. This has pleased teachers, particularly those who do

not realize that the quiet is there because, in the words of one, 'mobile phones have taken over the classroom'.

About 90 per cent of all university students possess such a phone and a majority of these receive and answer text messages during their classes. Hence the quiet that now reigns, where before there was chaos. Those teachers who notice are irate, but students polled defend themselves saying that, after all, they themselves are the only ones who suffer and should not consequently be scolded, even when they use their *keitai* for passing answers back and forth during examinations.

There is, additionally, the possibility of the contraption ringing. This distraction is much disliked the world over but in Japan, where it signals the social vice of 'selfishness', it is particularly hated, at least by the older generation. A recent Tokyo survey of pressing gripes revealed that number one was convenience-phone conversations in public places. Found particularly scandalous was such a phone going off in the Diet Chamber while the Emperor was delivering the opening message. The result was embarrassment and a reprimand.

It was indeed the second such, following the revelation that many Diet members were watching their screens and catching up on their e-mail instead of paying attention to the proceedings. As one commentator said: 'The only thing that distinguished them from high-school kids was that, as far as I could observe, no one was playing games.' Another report seemed more discouraged than irate. 'Given the state of the Diet, surely nobody would find issue with legislators who doze or exchange mail via cell phones, would they?'

With ringing cell phones now ubiquitous, trains run announcements pleading with passengers to limit phone use. Concert halls have tried pre-concert requests with no appreciable results

and are now building electronic shields, which it is hoped will keep out telephone signals. Suntory Hall, which hosts some four hundred concerts annually and which was recently embarrassed by a beeper piercing a Beethoven adagio during a Claudio Abbado concert, installed its shield in 1999. Not many other halls have followed its example but this is because the Japanese government is reluctant to permit radio wave blocking and so such permission is very difficult to obtain.

On the other hand it is very easy to get permission to install a relay antenna system in buildings that are too high, or too low, to receive the necessary frequencies. With mobile subscribers now topping seventy million, the systems have become basic infrastructure, like running water and electricity. Mitsubishi Real Estate Co. recently made all of its thirty buildings in the Tokyo metropolitan area cell-phone capable. High costs were jointly shouldered by the firm and by the local mobile phone giant, NTT DoCoMo, Inc.

There is also a small but growing demand for an invention said to be still on sale in Singapore, a laser cell-phone stopper. It is no longer available in Japan (one of the products was imaginatively called TelCut) since unlicensed use of jamming devices is an offence punishable by a maximum one-year prison term or a rather large fine. And, to be sure, no one knows what would happen if a pacemaker got hit instead. Still, the temptation is there – one push of the jammer button and the talking into one's palm ceases.

However, there may be long-range benefits for everyone. As Judith Martin has reminded us: 'Look what technology has already done for us. The telephone rescued us from the drop-in visit. The answering machine rescued us from the telephone. The beeper rescued us from having to check the answering machine. The cellular telephone rescued us from the beeper.'

In Japan the portable phone has indeed made the country a much more friendly-seeming place. Heretofore the Japanese have become well known for their chosen social aspect – neutral, incommunicative, famous as 'the subway face'. Unlike in Thailand, no one here spoke of the 'Japanese' smile. That was, however, before the portable phone.

Now, all over the country, millions of Japanese in the trains, on the street, in the subway itself, are smiling and laughing, bubbling with good humour, bowing with pleasure while earnestly spilling personal matters into unintended ears.

The inattentive foreign visitor might feel he had landed in the friendliest, the most demonstrative land on earth – everyone smiling and bowing politely, usually agreeing with whatever is said. Closer attention, however, would reveal that all of these pleasant greetings are not for him. Indeed, he is even more than usually invisible, because such good will is now aimed exclusively only at the palm of the pleasant person's hand wherein nestles the *keitai denwa*.

If the foreigner is in a position to understand the language being shouted around him, he will be impressed with not only its predominant conciliatory tone but also by its obvious geographical concern. One social commentator recently noted that ten years ago the phrase heard most often on the street was *sumimasen* (excuse me), but that now it is *ima doko?* (where are you now?).

Personal portable communication is also now ubiquitous. The media critic Kawabata Kenji recently discovered that over sixty million Japanese (one person out of two) have mobile phones. This compares with ownership rates in other industrialized nations but the differences occasioned are perhaps more noticeable in Japan since the results have been sudden – as, for example, the instant leap (or fall) from the reserved, closed, uncommunicative face to the open, voluble, chattering one.

The number of such phones can only grow as more and more uses are discovered. One such, much written about in the weeklies, is its role in the promotion of adultery. One wife (the reports are usually about wives, rarely about husbands) admitted that if she hadn't owned a mobile phone she would never have seriously considered being unfaithful to her husband. And yet, even if adultery is not indeed committed, it is said that long-term relationships are weakened.

One critic noticed that having a cell phone means you are 'connected', in that you can stay in touch with a number of people. At the same time, he notes, communication between men and women is becoming worse. Couples, ears to phone, make no effort to actually meet. One Tokyo woman stated that it was simply stupid for people to tie themselves down by actually meeting when they could keep 'in touch' by *keitai denwa*.

It has been suggested, found educator Janet Ashby, that the problem can be traced back 'to young parents raised on television who are deficient in face-to-face communication skills and have passed that shallow communication style on to their children'.

Consequently there is a growing number of people who have problems forming long-term intimate relationships. Since, as an Osaka regional news editor has said, 'Japanese are generally shy and poor at forming personal ties', both the portable phone and the internet tend to exacerbate the problem. In a sense no one any longer needs deep personal ties, not if one has a whole phone-full of acquaintances with whom to catch up and keep in touch. Such social promiscuity acts as security in much the same way that friendship used to. The difference, however, is in the respective durability of these two kinds of communication. I recently saw a young couple out on a date. Each was talking to someone else on portable phones – or maybe they were talking to each other.

However, if the individual in Japan experiences difficulty in forging friendships, he or she is uncommonly skilled in joining associations. Though people on a date have difficulty in talking to each other, people in a group do not. Particularly if they have a bond – the office group, the school group, the hobby group.

In a way the cell phone is a badge of belonging, and the number of other cell-phone numbers you can display is an indication of popularity. To see young people now is to watch them watching their *keitai denwa*. Perhaps they are counting friends, seeing who has called, wondering who themselves to call. In any event each is feeling the warmth of social closeness, the enveloping protection of the group, their 'family'. Particularly now that the close-knit Japanese family is no more, the *keitai denwa* may be seen as a kind of time machine which will return the user to an earlier, happier, more close-knit time.

One critic interviewed a young *keitai*-wielding woman named Yuko and found that her cell-phone memory stored nearly three hundred phone numbers but only fifty or so, she says, were friends. The rest belonged to casual acquaintances, many of them people whose faces she cannot even recall.

This is because Yuko, in efforts to build a large and popular group, gives her number out to strangers. 'When I get picked up and the boy asks my number, I usually give it because it's just too much trouble to refuse.'

This can then lead to complications. Strangers can be a bother. Rebuffed, they give your number to the kind of people you would not want to be friends with. Also there are bullying e-mail messages, from whom one does not know. One girl interviewed is much troubled by her *keitai* promiscuity. She gets all sorts of unwanted calls. 'Of course, I haven't told my boyfriend about this. When I feel like just having a good cry I call my friends and they make me feel a little better.'

The susceptible can fall into even worse hands. A criminally minded individual may be on the other end of the line. He calls and hangs up after one ring. Since you now have his number and are curious you call back. That means he now has your number verified and suddenly you are in the ring for sex-related services. NTT DoCoMo says it receives some five hundred complaints a month.

But none of the Japanese young would for a second consider relinquishing their convenience phones. If they did they would be deprived of the individuality that keeps them melded into a group. And this individuality is guarded.

The individuality may be augmented as well. Though all *keitai denwa* are the same each must be decorated personally, since the object is, among other things, status-symbolizing. It has become a personal icon of pop culture. Hence the amazing variety of straps for sale, the diversity of icons (Mickey and Minnie, Hello Kitty, Superman, Barbie), and the melange of ringing tones. These used to be simple irritating electronic bells. No longer – as the *keitai* boom continues all sorts of new articles attach to it like barnacles.

Social critic Steve McClure has outlined some of the latest. Downloadable ringing tones, now called *chakumero* (derived from *chakushin*, arrival), come in all shapes and sizes but they are derived from the pop tunes that seemingly change daily. While Japan is not alone in downloading pop tunes for ringing tones, no other country has gone further with the idea. *Chakumero* websites not only list endless selections, they also feature step-by-step instructions on how to key a *chakumero* into your *keitai*.

With each phone securely personalized the owner may feel a kind of individuality within the same uniformity of impersonal collectivity. This is popular everywhere but is perhaps more widespread in Japan. At any rate no other country makes less use of that evolved cell phone which, instead of bursting into song, merely vibrates.

There is no need to. Japan has a long tradition of public neglect. The individual may be as obnoxious as he pleases, though within his group such behaviour must be modulated to that standard – even if they are all using noisy portable phones. Besides this, traditional manners are visibly eroding. Not only are keitai used for inadvertently broadcasting the most personal of manners, one now applies make-up on the street and even openly eats on the street as well.

This was never done when Japan was still an integrated society: no eating, no kissing, no loud talking, much less the continual braying into the cell phone. It is only in the last ten years that this (a collapse of traditional freedom, a breakthrough into something more like public individuality) has been visible. It is a spectacular indication of the end of the old.

At the same time that they gorge on *Ginza*, collide in mute random, and are forever shouting into their phones, one could also say that the young are also learning individuality. No longer are they victims of the mass. Rather, they are learning how to stand out. And no longer being fearful of outside opinion means something.

Maybe. But watch these people as they work their *keitai*. Or is it the other way around? Are their *keitai* working them? As far as the eye can see, people are either talking into their machines or staring at them, or warily checking them – to see if they have any messages, to reassure themselves that, individual though they may be, they are not alone. And notice the seriousness, the earnestness with which they continually check their social temperatures. A spare moment and out comes the phone from pocket or purse. And with it an oddly serious expression. This is not merely a communication machine, it is also a guru, a higher authority.

The more convenient our society becomes, the more we lose our sense of being part of it. Now anyone outside the magic circle of friends is considered of small importance. Yet this social life is fragile. Sometimes the Japanese will e-mail each other to ask if it is all right to phone. Indeed, so much time is spent in communicating itself that there is no time left to communicate anything.

Kosupure

Kosupure is a portmanteau term taken from 'costume play'. *Pure* indicates diversion, as in the popular *sekusupure* – play identifies, renders acceptable and differentiates.

What *kosupure* differentiates from is serious costuming. Japan remains the land where all cooks wear cook hats, where travellers to the nearest snow-covered hill wear full skiing costume, and where the clothing most often indicates the profession or the activity. This is serious because Japan remains a land where classes are, just as in the Tokugawa period, to be identified. Hence, even now, students wear uniforms (boys and girls alike) and visible employees (such as females in department stores) wear identical dress. When costuming is not serious, however, then it is play, and the definition becomes that of the standard English dictionary: 'A style of dress characteristic of a particular country, period, or people, often worn in a play or at a masquerade.'

A relatively recent occurrence, *kosupure* is dressing up in public, being someone (or something) else. Other countries are familiar with this. Halloween, for example, provides an excuse to dress up, wear outlandish costumes, appear completely different. It occurs once a year and this in the West seems sufficient. In Japan, however, *kosupure* occurs once a week: on Sundays, at a prime location, for example in Tokyo at Harajuku, the home of teen fashion. The neighbourhood resonates with green hair, blue lips, stained faces, fantasy frocks of various kinds, 'blood'-stained bandages, shrouds.

There are a number of themes running through the throng. One is the monstrous aspect favoured by horror-rock bands such as Malice Mizer, or the now defunct X-Japan, a rock group famous for its radical hair, costumes and make-up. But there are others as well, including costume-imitations from beloved fantasy films, impersonations of favourite teenage singers, and a discreet amount of cross-dressing.

Like Halloween, the weekly *kosupure* get-togethers serve a number of functions. There is the atmosphere of carnival and the consequent temporary lifting of rules and regulations. There is the licence to dabble in the forbidden. And there is the freedom to be, for a time, someone else.

Perhaps this last has the greatest appeal in Japan, a country where how you dress is who you are. Many observers have noted the unusual number of uniforms worn seriously. Those forced on students, from kindergarten to university, on company employees, on service workers. Even when not enforced these are adopted: the toed socks, jodhpured trousers, fancy neckbands favoured by construction workers, for example.

In the country where the identification of the name card is always necessary, a sartorial detection kit is also required. It is assumed that clothes make the man. This is a supposition some-

times shared. The world over soldiers are put into uniform – the costume, by definition, kills. At the same time, since you are what you wear, you can be someone else if you wear something different.

This is commonly thought of as, at worst, shady. In traditional Japan it was sporadically forbidden that samurai visit the licensed quarter. Hence it became traditional for the cruising warrior to leave his swords at home and wear a large sedge hat which partially obscured his face. Everyone recognized the costume but it was agreed that all would also respect it. Here was just an anonymous figure and not a samurai breaking his own law. Sometimes a simple head-cloth tied under the nose to hide the mouth was sufficient. It was understood that this was 'disguise'.

With deception thus acknowledged it should be no surprise that in Japan frivolity has a certain sanction. It is understood that periods of foolishness are necessary and this celebration of the trifling, the futile, the silly has its place. It even has a name. *Matsuri* is usually translated as 'festival', and so it is. At the same time this festival spirit is also celebrated as heedless and thoughtless. If the origins are in religion, the spirit possessions of Shinto, the modern-day manifestations have secularized into an approved activity where lack of purpose (other than display) is a motivation.

Historically, such manifestations of *matsuri* have long been a part of Japan. The most spectacular, and the largest, occurred during a troubling time when Western influences were first making serious inroads into conventional Japanese mores during the mid-nineteenth century. Bands of dancing citizenry flocked, chanting the mantra of the new frivolity, a single 'word' – *Eijanaika!* It meant something like 'everything's OK, right?' and implied an extreme toleration.

It countered the repressive Meiji government, which was insisting that just everything was definitely not all right. Indeed, the new government had as many rules as did the Tokugawa government before it. That the new rules were supposedly liberal (cut off your topknot, don't wear kimono, eat meat) made them no less draconian. It was in reaction to this clamp-down that these frivolous bands began clogging the roads of urban Japan.

Eijanaika, eijanaika, eijanaika, they chanted as they danced through the streets, their mindless mantra affirming nothing less than chaos because that is what it would be if just everything was OK. This apparently spontaneous instance of civil disobedience was indeed a kind of revolution, but behind it lay Japan's long licence. A season of frivolity was allowed.

The dancers were soon squelched but the fact that they had appeared at all argues for an unusual governmental tolerance for frivolity. Rome had its Saturnalia, the European medieval period saw various celebrations of legal licence, but these were regulated, looked forward to, disposed of when they were over. A festival is called a riot only when it is spontaneous.

If one is surprised that such could occur in Japan, always the most paternally governed of nations, one should remember that Japan had also the most provocation to throw off this paternalism. That it has never successfully done so does not argue that there is a less felt need.

It is ironic that the expression of this discontent used the very means that had been governmentally sponsored. Edo, no less than Rome, used festivals as a safety measure, a way to allow the populace to let off steam. The spirit of *matsuri* expressed kept the populace in line. And yet here with the *eijanaika* folk the *matsuri* spirit was raging, out of control, across the land – for a time.

Now firmly in control, this and successive government cabinets have all seen the need for a pliant populace, kept that way from time to time by allowing it out to play. One of the reasons for fostering a public addicted to gambling (pachinko) and to drugs (the tobacco industry, 'formerly' governmental), as well as being purposely exposed to the delights of a legally uncontrolled sex industry, is just that such makes good citizens: pliant, mollified, unwilling to stand up and be counted or going around stopping bucks.

While *kosupure* ranks low among instances of civil disobedience, something like this is encouraged as an antibody to something presumably more serious, such as a revolution or a general strike. The political uses of matsuri are smoothed over and the frivolity enhanced. At the same time the public is led to believe that something is being expressed publicly.

While most adults seem to be inured to being what they seem (Hallowe'en worldwide is merely a kids' holiday) the Japanese young still have hopes for some experimentation before settling down to middle-aged selfhood. One can *épater la bourgeoisie* to whom one actually belongs by wearing bloody bandages or appearing in a black lace see-through dress just like that worn by your favourite cross-dressing rock star. Or one can wear the garb of favourite comic-book heroes, with imitation samurai swords, wannabe karate outfits. More rarely seen, however, are one-of-a-kind costumes.

Thus, sartorial statements are generic and similarity is achieved amidst a perceived diversity. Also, shocking or antagonizing, or even amusing, is not the real aim. Eric Prideaux reports being told by the manager of one of the boutiques around Japan specializing in costumes that 'it's a tool for breaking the ice. With just one look you can figure out a person's interests, no

introductions necessary'. Among the fifty thousand weekly customers whom the costumiers can count on, a major interest centres around *manga, anime,* computer games – dressing up like the heroes or heroines. Thus one's taste in Japanese pop is indicated at once.

The reason for such a seemingly superficial preference is given by Professor Masahiro Yamada, as reported by Michael Hoffman. 'The age of lifetime friendship is over, what young people want from their friends nowadays is the assurance that they are not alone. For that just about anyone will do, and the key to being, or seeming, part of a crowd is to maintain a studied vacuity. It's everywhere, beneath the garish make-up.'

Cosmetics play a large role in both *kosupure* and in ordinary everyday make-up. This enormous industry (the world's second largest) targets not only women and adolescent girls but also men and children. Aiming at girls under twelve, companies send make-up consultants to the toy sections of department stores to teach little girls how to use cosmetics under the slogan 'You Will Be a Lady Starting Today'. This has resulted in a new generation of *kosume* (cosmetic) kids. The consequences have been successful. One drugstore chain noted that nearly half of the shoplifters apprehended were still in primary school.

Yet, despite commercial encouragement, despite peer pressure, despite the desperate timidity behind all of this, there is something else in this safe if public display. The insistence of the young in doing things their way is there even if the things themselves are conformist and standardized. As Brian McVeigh has said: 'What many Japanese do with the codes of dress uniformity – alter, supplement, subvert, convert and make cute – illustrates an adaptable, abounding and resolute (indeed, at times obstinate) individuality.'

Being self-centred (*jiko-chushinteki*) is not anywhere considered a civic virtue, it being to society's benefit to discourage this, but small amounts may be used as innoculation against something even worse. This has long been known in Japan where its various governments, though bristling with prohibitions, have carefully refused to censor sexuality as such, and have always kept *matsuri* in a special category.

It still does. The Japanese spirit of frivolity is an embodiment of impotence, an inability to create actual social change and hence an attempt to mimic it. Dancing in the streets or prancing about in costume is equally frivolous in that it cannot be serious, since to be serious is to have some effect, and it is carefully seen to that *eijanaika* posturing and *kosupure* posing alike have no social effect whatsoever.

Fake Foreigners

Well over a hundred years ago Lafcadio Hearn showed a number of pictures of Western young women to some Japanese acquaintances. Always interested in perceptions of beauty, he wanted to see how such exoticisms as yellow hair, white skin and blue eyes appeared to them. Their reactions, according to Marc Keane, who has recounted the incident, were uniform. 'The faces are nice', said the Japanese, 'all except the eyes. The eyes are too big, the eyes are monstrous'.

Now, more than a century later, the Japanese no longer find Western eyes monstrous. Indeed, for some years now young women have undergone surgery to have the epicanthic folds removed from their eyelids, used mascara and liner to render them large and lustrous, even occasionally used sky-blue contact lens to emulate the once scorned orbs from abroad.

Hearn would have been much interested in this. Changes during a century are to be expected but such a reversal is unusual. What to make of it – particularly when it is seen in the context of all the other mutations in the Japanese attitude toward things foreign.

Hair, for example. Until recently Japanese hair was uniformly black, occasionally with a slightly brownish tint that occasioned much embarrassment for the young people genetically possessing it. There was, indeed, a whole literature devoted to the virtues of straight, black hair.

However, as the editor of the Japanese edition of *Vogue* has said, such relentless similarity 'gave young Japanese a complex. We're short, have the same colour eyes and couldn't change the colour of our hair. Now we can change height, eyes, hair.'

Indeed, dyeing and peroxiding is common. And not only brown, though that chestnut shade known as *chapatsu* is perhaps most popular. Platinum blonde, red, pink, even blue and green abound. The Pola Cultural Center (run by a cosmetic company) produced a study finding that more than half of the nation's women between fifteen and sixty-five dyed their hair. It did not count the men.

Obviously a major change of attitude has occurred; and not only in the multi-hued wearers themselves. Authorities, usually the first to complain of such social irregularities, do so no longer. A spokesman for the Bank of Tokyo-Mitsubishi said it does not mind a hair-dyed staff so long as customers do not complain. The Tokyo Metropolitan Government's Office of Education said that if a teacher (and presumably a student) wished to dye her or his hair, the principal 'might have to give approval.' Law enforcement agencies agree – the National Personnel Authority, a governmental agency, said that it too had no authority in this matter. 'After all, those in charge of a particular workplace have the final say on coloured hair.'

So, no one is complaining at the promiscuous hues, and

pop stars and sports heroes now regularly wear hair other than black. Singer Amuro Namie helped start the fad with her bronze-coloured locks, and now athletic heroes sport tinted locks. Baseball slugger Tsuyoshi is sandy coloured, top pitcher Matsuzaka Daisuke is gold, and soccer superstar Nakata Hidetoshi is carrot-topped.

Along with mutating hair colour, also to be observed is augmented height. Just as the abandonment of black hair indicates a major infringement of the homogeneous picture Japan used to push, so the wish to be tall challenges a belief formerly insisted upon – that the Japanese are a short people. Though seats in new auditoriums are routinely made too small, and large kids cannot find large sizes, the new ethos not only acknowledges that the Japanese are a big people but also that they want to be bigger.

Today's teenagers indeed are often taller than their parents. The fish/rice diet has given way to hamburger/french fries, and kneeling on the *tatami* (which is said to have kept the legs short) is no longer practised since there is scarcely any of that floor covering left, at least not where the young congregate. And they want to be taller still.

This wish has been around for a time. A big film star of the fifties, Ishihara Yujiro, younger brother of the present Governor of Tokyo, got by on his long legs. Such a desire was, however, a male province. Japanese women were supposed to be short. Now new is that the young woman wants to be taller as well.

This desire has been apparent for several seasons in the stockings worn by high-school girls. These thick, woollen socks (called 'elephant socks' by the disapproving) bunch around the shins and are supposed, by contrast, to make the limbs appear both longer and more slender. The main purpose is a hopeful elimination of the 'piano leg' look, long a bane, real or fancied,

of the female Japanese adolescent. Even now, elephant socks sell well, each pair with its little tube of glue to make certain it bunches at just the right place.

More recently, however, the desire for heightened eminence resulted in a new kind of footwear. These were shoes with skyscraper soles (*atsuzoko sandaru*), some of them up to ten inches (25 centimetres) deep, on top of which teenagers teetered down the fashionable avenues of Shibuya, Harajuku and Omote-sando.

To be sure, such elevated footwear was not entirely new. In old Japan the licensed quarter was seasonally diverted by a great procession of very expensive courtesans wearing platform *zori* sandals so high that a kind of wading, weaving step was necessary to progress at all. This, however, was actually a sign of ostentatious consumption. It was the patron who paid for all this. Like foot-binding, it was really a glorification of ownership.

Not now. No one owned these tall, platinum-haired young women, their blue contact lenses twinkling. They were plainly in command of themselves – even if that command was sometimes a bit unsteady. A survey by Aoba Gakuen women's college indicated that one in four students had fallen off their elevated footwear, half of these suffering fractures and 'other injuries'.

There were other dangers, as well. The Osaka Municipal Police banned such footwear while the wearer was at the wheel since there were a number of auto accidents, some of them fatal, all caused by platform shoes.

However, a little bit of danger never stopped a fashion. Arguably just as hazardous was the fad for a tan so extreme that the chestnut-tressed person seemed made of mahogany. The look was a product of many long hours in the tanning 'salons', places unbothered by police inspection. After word of skin cancer surfaced, however, the 'natural' tanning of the skin was replaced by various stains and dyes which, judiciously applied, created much the same effect.

So there she was, the new Japanese girl, her hair a frosty lemon or a pure platinum, her eyes sparkling blue or green, her skin a dark Palm-Beach hue, her skirt micro-mini, her encrusted fingernails glittering, her legs long and her height imposing. Isn't there something familiar about her?

Then we recognize her. Barbie! – a walking, living Barbie doll, that beloved American kitsch emblem, that adored icon for all that is trashy, here, alive, walking down 'Killer Avenue' in Tokyo's Shibuya. The close resemblance was acknowledged. Naito Minoru, fashion commentator, wrote that 'one of the hottest trends among Japanese girls this year has been to look like Barbie'.

This trend was, like most others, commercially inspired. In the fashion-crazed district of Shibuya in Tokyo there are a vast number of boutiques, some of which have an enormous clout with the shopping young. Mainly housed in the 109 Building, at present a mecca for the fashionable, are a number of boutiques, several of which sell ¥100 million worth of outfits a month. One such, named Egoist, at present the most popular, was looking around for new images for the clueless young. Barbie had just had an anniversary in the land of her birth and that seemed reason enough to introduce her into Japan. Not the doll itself, it was already there, just the look.

Salesgirls, here the first to dress up in new fashions and display them at Egoist and other outlets, perfected the look and then displayed the results. The consequences were apparently instantaneous. Arata Hiroko, connected with a rival chain, A-Girl Co., complained that girls promptly passed this latest buzz on their hand phones and it soon became a boom. Barbie after Barbie tottered out onto the streets, followed by Ken after Ken.

Fashion icons in Japan are rarely created from the top down. Though there are lots of fashion designers (Issei Miyake *et al*) it was not they who created the Barbie boom. Rather, a seller, or a group of them, consulted a public and together a craze was created. This kind of social creation has been called the 'percolator' model, as differentiated from the 'drip' model.

When 'Yasu' Nakasone, then prime minister of Japan, called on his great pal 'Ron' Reagan, then president of the United States, and they 'hammered out' an accord, Ron simply told his subordinates what to do and, despite the filters of Congress and the House of Representatives, the plan dripped down into accomplished fact. Yasu, however, had a different kind of pot. Here the constituency has to be persuaded to circulate and this it often fails to do, the Diet becoming then a cauldron of conflicting currents.

That governmental decision and fashion agreement should share a process indicates that social structure in Japan is neither the paternal dictatorship that the right would prefer nor the 'democracy' advocated by the left. It is indeed something else. The percolator produced Barbie in Japan.

However, as is well known, Japan always perfects an acquisition from abroad, and shortly the Barbie-look was Japanified. The method is explained by Stuart Braun. Interviewing one of these fashion-makers he was told: 'We Japanese have very good editing skills. We get bits and pieces from all over the world and digest it, put it through the filter, and then output it as a new style that fits our culture.' He was then given the names of a few of the latest (Spring 2002) trends: 'bohemian, ethnic, tyrolean knit, cyber trance, used touch, resort, relax, and cute conservative'.

A problem, however, is that by the time a new style is announced it is already old-fashioned. There are some 800 new fashion designs a year created by the endless demand of youthful fashion fans. The editor of *Popteen*, a magazine which sells up to 500,000 copies a month, says that 'by the time the magazines comes out, the fashion has already changed, things move so fast. There is no constant, the only strategy is to keep changing.' Thus a lot of what the young in America are now wearing was reinterpreted, remodelled and discarded by Japan's youth half a year ago. Consequently to even write of fashion is to deal with the past.

One of the results of this remarkable turnover was the now-vanished *ganguro* (black-face) look, so named by those who did not like it. The tan was more intense, very dark brown indeed, the eye make-up now created a teddy-bear look. Journalist Jacinta Koch has described the full effect. The 'white-eyed bleach-blonde' effect is augmented by the *ganguro* outfits: 'vinyl jackets, sequinned, shiny, feathered and animal prints; bright and shimmering colours in hot pink, blue, orange, with sexy black jackets, accompanied by a *ganguro* boyfriend with bleach-blond hair, fake tan and a hotted-up love van.'

All this was apparently the work of Nakane Reiko, Egoist's most famous employee. She has the in-store title of 'Charisma Sales Clerk' and embodies a 'push-the-limits fashion sense'. The black-face look certainly did that. Its appeal was articulated by Nakane herself when she said, 'It's embarrassing to go out with your face naked. I think a face looks firmer and cuter when it's dark. And it's great for a woman to look beautiful. It makes her feel more confident.' Except that not everyone would call black face beautiful, though perhaps it appeared so compared to later excesses.

The black-face look then morphed into the *yamamba* look. The term means 'old mountain hag' and now the tresses were grey, the hair was ratted, and the teddy-bear eyes had became panda-like. The usual fashion transformation has occurred (the beautiful becomes ugly and consequently ugly is beautiful) and there seems no further way to push this trend. It is over and, as I write, black-faced beauties totter o'er Harajuku no more.

It was, however, by no means the first time that Japanese skin colour had been augmented (or diminished). Just as 'unnatural' as the black-face look was the fashion for whitening the face, for shaving the eyebrows, for blackening the teeth.

From as early as the seventh century, white powder was used on the faces and other body parts of the upper classes. By the Heian period it was agreed that a lady of quality had fair skin, hence her staying in the dark house most of the time, and all the drapes and coverings employed when she went out. It was the weather-beaten peasant's wife who was properly dark. Since nature does not observe such social niceties, however, quantities of mercury chloride and white lead were imported from China in order to create a beauty aid which was mixed with water and thickly applied with a brush, rendering an aristocratic fairness. By the seventeenth century the practice was popular in all classes that could afford it and was usually restricted to women. The resulting lead poisoning was responsible for more deaths than any accidents caused by stilt-shoes, and after 1870 the government banished the ingredients and eventually the whitening power itself.

The long fad for whitened faces not only meant that these women were rich enough not to work outside, it also suggested a resemblance to those from abroad who were, to the Japanese of the time, routinely perceived as progressive. If one accepts that the traditional white-face constituted a kind of entitlement, then the more recent black-face could be read as kindred identification, but this time with people of colour, particularly those who had already so influenced Japanese popular culture through hip-hop clothing and soul music.

Among the female aristocracy during the Heian period eyebrows were routinely removed. They were perceived as ugly. Sei Shonagon, writing *circa* 1000, has a line in her *Pillow Book* describing them as 'worms'. The depilation, a ritual known as *okimayu*, not only made a woman attractive, it also denoted that she had come of age. New ones were then painted higher up on the face and these were perceived as beautiful.

Another sign of the coming of age, from the twelfth century on, was *ohaguro*, or tooth-blackening. A mixture of ferrous oxide, tea and sake was used to colour the teeth, resulting in the black hole perceived as not only beautiful but healthy for the teeth. Originally both sexes blackened and many a samurai redid his teeth before going into battle. By the eighteenth century, however, its use was confined to women and indicated that the black-mouthed beauty was already married. Tanizaki Jun'ichiro, in praising shadows, particularly stresses the alluring beauty of the darkly toothless mouth, but as early as 1873 the empress of Japan, Meiji's wife, had indicated otherwise by refusing *ohaguro*.

One of the uses of such cosmetic extremes was the definition of women as chattels, to be disposed of as men saw fit. But another, diametrically opposed, was that of empowering women through definition. Here black face meets white face and panda eyes meet no eyebrows. The modern trend is definitely intended to empower women.

Popular TV commentator Nakamura Usagi, looking at all the big eyes on the young, recently offered a reason. Remembering that in the Heian period beauty consisted of small, slit-like eyes, and seeing that only the ferocious Nio, guardian deities, and

Hannya, the female demon in the Noh, had such large, glaring eyes, she reasons that big eyes were symbols of terror rather than beauty in traditional Japan – the reaction, you will remember, of Lafcadio Hearn's early viewers.

'To be stared at by large eyes is a terror-inspiring experience for us Japanese', said Nakamura. The current fashion for them is thus ambivalent since 'the uneasy feeling we have when stared at by someone is not one of love but fear'. Yet stared at we are by big-eyed, stilted, tanned, blonde-maned young females. Japanese are now much more receptive to such 'baleful influence. If today's Japan conceives [such] eyes as beautiful, then our nation's ego has really gone weak.' Indeed, the icon for power thus created is apparent. The girls are taller, more confident – and, along with everything else, go a loud brassy voice and a braying laugh. It is a successful creation in that it achieved what it intended, but its parentage was not merely Barbie in bed with Hello Kitty.

In many cultures, it has been noted, classes on the rise pull themselves up through a kind of imitation of where they have come from. In upwardly mobile America, as we have seen, middle-class men wear lumberjack shirts of low-class rural origin and even upper-class couples dress like children (snow suits, sun outfits) of the middle class they have presumably left. There are, however, differences.

As Thorstein Veblen early noted, the utility of both conspicuous leisure and consumption in the creation of reputability lies in 'the element of waste that is common to both, in the one case it is a waste of time and effort, in the other it is a waste of goods.' In having their hair expensively arranged in 'corn rows' or frizzed into equally expensive 'dreadlocks' Americans imitate a former lower state (in some cases, slaves) and at the same time, since the hair style is so expensive, reach the level of conspicuous waste. Thus, this new version of the corn-row hairdo empowers the wearer because he or she can afford it.

Seen in Japan, however, the corn row and the dreadlock can be read only as waste because there is no nexus (Black Power), and because so much time, effort and money has been expanded to such small result. It is just this, however, which often constitutes the attraction – like the gold flakes on the sushi fleetingly seen during Japan's short-lived 'bubble' years.

Traditionally women had few empowering choices. One of them, however, is a particularly rebellious-seeming look. Girls imitate the appearance of their fallen but liberated sisters. This is the 'whore' look – never called that. Often indeed it has no name. One remembers the anonymous American beehive hairdo of several decades ago, copied from European prostitutes but never acknowledging this fact.

I do not wish to suggest that Barbie is a prostitute, but I would submit that such an image is not antithetical to the ambitions of girls on their way toward empowerment. Nor, indeed, is prostitution itself. The local media is still reeling from revelations that some 'high-school girls' have taken money for *enjo kosai* (delicately translated as 'compensated dating') and gone the whole way for the money. Desire for a Gucchi or Fendi handbag is often mentioned as reason for the downfall.

A national conference of parent-teacher associations conducted a recent survey, reported on by journalist Tim Large, which discovered that only about six in every thousand high-school girls were actually involved. Of course this is six too many, say the critics, but such a small percentage should not, it seems, encourage the media to make this much of it.

Yet it does – and this influences readers, male ones. Another survey, by the Tokyo Gakugei University, disclosed that 75 per cent of its girl students had been approached by media-crazed older men, and that 50 per cent had been offered compensation for a date. Pickings must have been slim for them in that, according to the survey, only one out of 170 girls thus approached agreed.

Nonetheless, the public at large (and not just dirty old men) see the new liberated look as deplorable. The girls are called *kogyaru*, a term not intended as a compliment, and 'reform' is attempted. Few, however, are concerned about the plight that the young women are also expressing through their finery.

One who takes them seriously is fashion-illustrator Masuyama Hiroshi, whose popular likenesses of the dressed-up *kogyaru* usually show them with tears in their eyes. 'The conventional image is that these girls are all carefree, self-indulgent, doing whatever they want', he said. 'But, actually, they are feeling a lot of distress.'

Often alienated from their parents, marginalized by their schools, criticized by the press, many still see the *kogyaru* image as a means of freedom, even notoriety, before a future of married drudgery and certain obscurity. They will never again be so appealing, never again at liberty so to 'express' themselves.

They live entirely in the present, says Masuyama, and have no other models than pop stars and store clerks. As the popular Amuro Namie, spokesperson for her generation, sang: 'I don't know how to be a girl.' These young women, continues Masuyama 'are as stunted and moulded as *bonsai*'. Further, the media is to blame for their alleged licentiousness. 'By simultaneously glorifying and condemning the *kogyaru* lifestyle, it places a heavy emotional burden on these young shoulders.'

Perhaps this is one of the reasons why these girls (and boys) are so willing to experiment with their images, trying on this and that in hopes of a fit. Perhaps, having discovered that nothing made in Japan fits them, they are looking to the land of Barbie.

There is some evidence that this is so. Social psychologist Sakaki Hirobumi told Eric Prideaux that the speed with which Japan picks up and drops trends is indicative of a social climate currently much tougher than people are used to, as well as of both massive uncertainty and a new desire for change. A shift from conformity to innovation is necessary 'if Japan is to compete in a rapidly changing global market'.

The young are looking for 'mini-gurus', like Nakane Reiko with her big hair and large eyes. The young are always, everywhere, in need of role-models but these seem in particularly short supply in Japan. Some critics say that Japan is now experiencing simply an acerbation of an old trend. This 'is an inevitable result of the ethnic self-denial that has suffused Japanese society ever since the Meiji era, and especially since the end of the Second World War', according to sociologist Sato Kenji.

Bent on achieving the social goals of both modernization and Westernization, the Japanese have sought, says Sato, to reject their own history and traditions. They have tried to become *Nihonjin-banare* (de-Japanized). This is an emotionally neutral term meaning one looks and acts more like a Westerner (particularly a Caucasian) than an average Japanese. And within its traditional confines the concept has been entertained if not encouraged.

Evidence abounds. When the Portuguese first came to Japan in the sixteenth century, their fashions were soon imitated. Japanese took to wearing capes, trousers, boots. When the Americans came in the nineteenth century the same thing occurred: top hats, bustles, buttoned shoes. And now, as we have seen, a new generation of fake foreigners has been spawned.

It has long been noted that store window mannikins are almost invariably 'Caucasian', and so 'foreigners' were showing Japanese what might look good to them. The looks of characters in both *manga* and *anime* are Western. In even so ethnic an entertainment as the cartoon *Princess Mononoke*, characters obviously intended to be Japanese still have long legs and big, wide eyes, features identical to presumably Caucasian characters in other big-hit animated cartoons.

It is said that this is the main ingredient in their popularity, that 'only anime, and its cousin manga, can convincingly meld Japanese and Caucasian attributes into a natural-looking human being.' These, continues Sato Kenji, 'are the only two media capable of portraying reality the way Japanese feel it should be.'

While all this has been read by foreign critics as a takeover, there is nothing sinister at work. Just as Portuguese fritters became *tempura*, just as French pork cutlets became *tonkatsu*, just as English becomes Janglish, so some Japanese take on the look of being foreigners.

Just the look. No more is possible nor desired. Things foreign are emulated, not the actuality of being foreign. Japan has fewer natives living abroad than almost any other major country.

The tottering, big-eyed, blonde parody on the street is like the equally foreign-appearing mannikin in the store window. Both are insisting upon – that great Japanese accomplishment – appearance as reality At the same time no one is taken in, nor is one supposed to be.

Look at me, I am fashionable, flashy, foreign, says the *kogyaru* and *kyoboi*. At the same time they are telling us that they are searching for an identity, any identity, even that of the fake foreigner.

Afterword

The urge to be the same, to safely conform, is often seen as a Japanese characteristic. The only way to be different is to be so within the permitted perimeter of a group, whose boundaries, though elastic, expand or contract only with permission of the group itself.

How different is this from other countries? Not much, but one difference is that no one denies the fact, unlike in such purportedly individualistic nations as the USA, where such denial is routine. In Japan, however, it is not only undenied, but insisted upon, this inclusive conformism. There is even a term for it – the *wa* is the circle of agreement within which a desirable social consensus is possible and without which an irregularity bordering on anarchy is threatened.

The *wa* becomes the consensus of harmony. It was the first article in the first 'constitution', that which was promulgated in AD 604 by Prince Shotoku, who is reported as saying: 'Harmony is to be valued.' Certainly, but to make it a law? Yes, and there are reasons. Among them is that it is easier for a ruler to control a harmonious people, and that all rulers have a vested interest in a peaceful populace.

In Japan, however, the probably innate and certainly inescapable human attraction to rivalry is all the stronger for having been so constitutionally denied. In actuality, *wa* remains an idea, not a fact. It is an ideal to be aspired to, not a goal which has been attained. It constitutes an ideology – an invisible one. The controlled but apparent rivalry between rulers and ruled seen in a more demotic state is interiorized in Japan.

The noble ideal of *wa* is enthroned, but that upon which it rests is ignored – hence squabbles over seating privilege in the Diet, hence bitter neighbourhood quarrels, households battling over the etiquette of putting out the garbage. So intense is rivalry in Japan that one might suggest that the concept of *wa* had to be invented because rivalry itself is seen only as disorder.

Rivalry is a fact, it is by nature biological, consequently so is human disorder. Yet, in Japan, the problematical aspects of the biological are rarely acknowledged and seldom allowed to show themselves. Unruly nature is traditionally tamed. Like the Japanese garden, like the bonsai tree, the potentially unruly populace is trained into belief in the *wa*. 'Rivalry, traditionally feared as disorder, is driven underground, its creative potential sapped', observes Michael Hoffman in his analysis of the phenomenon.

Everyone loves peace and envisions Utopia but why then has Japan taken so stern a stand. One of the reasons is that it has had a history of century-long civil *wars*. Another is the fact that what is damned gains force. And yet another is that the *wa* needs concern itself only with the present – there is no past *wa* worth mentioning, and it is not possible in Japanese to formulate a future for anything, let alone *wa*.

The Japanese language has no equivalent to 'will' or 'shall' because there is no future tense. Consequently the Japanese have no intention that must be expressed in such a tense. Aims are seen in a present-tense form. Lacking a future tense, Japanese traditionally believe only in present reality: *utsutsu*, that which is right before your eyes. Future and past alike tend to be seen as insignificant.

Terashima Shin'ichi has noted that, equally, there is no past in Japan. The past is not a completed stretch of time, rather it survives into the present. Certain aspects of the past are spoken of in the present tense, those which continue to be important to the speaker.

With the future unpronounceable and the past extending into the present, the Japanese language makes the present tense the only inhabitable one. Everything else is problematical. People save money because the future is opaque, they do not properly acknowledge *war*time deeds because these do not extend into an accepted present.

Many other peoples (depending upon their languages) really exist in three dimensions of time, but, for many in Japan, reality is only that which exists in the eternal present, not what happened in an unimportant past or an unimaginable future.

A like impoverishment, if that is what it is, has also been noted by Terashima. There are, he says, only two kinds of things in the Japanese world – those which are *honto* (real, true) and those which are *uso* (unreal, false). Consequently the present is real, objective, scientific, the past and the future are unreal because they are subjective and imaginary.

Correspondingly, Terashima continues, one's life also should be grounded in the present. Be on guard to maintain homogeneity, stay neither too far behind the group, nor too far ahead of it.

You must be unanimous in your perception of an accepted reality – the present.

Japan's policy of the present might in part account for the rapid turnover of fad and fashion. Everywhere, to be sure, fashion is perceived as new and 'old-fashioned' is rarely a term of praise. At the same time, the Japanese example exhibits a speed rare elsewhere. Change as a dynamic constant seems inconsistent with Japan's self-image as the home of tradition (Fuji, geisha, pagodas) but in actuality tradition is a very selective affair and, in any event, is contrived only to reassure and lend a fleeting identity to Japan in its will to change.

This change is rarely contested. It is, in fact, more often celebrated. The relationship between tradition and change in Japan, says Edward Seidensticker 'has always been complicated by the fact that change itself is a tradition.' One of the better-known markers of this accommodation of change is the aesthetic term *mono no aware*. Whatever else it might mean it always implies a positive acceptance of change. But in homely terms it is sighting one more grey hair, one more wrinkle, and – without a thought of the beauty parlour – registering approval that things are doing as they must and that this is good, because it is the *way* things are. Resignation turns dynamic and the very thing that might be seen as lessening is celebrated as empowering.

Perhaps, paradoxically, this is why the new is so welcomed in this country of permanently eroding tradition. Pico Iyer has noted that 'Japanese inventions have won over the world through their smallness, their precision and their elegant design – the very qualities that originally drew me to *haiku* and *tatami* rooms. The foreigner talks of contradiction and self-erosion but a

Japanese sees an ongoing, adaptable mix of native forms and borrowed traditions.'

A concern over the demise of old Japan may be one of 'Japan's most distinctive and evergreen traditions, especially as the country has always embraced the new and the foreign so eagerly. Keep things new and they always stay the same. Novelty is the oldest tradition.'

Imejicheinji: nothing changes except the image itself, put to social uses, to the stratification of status through the creation of an order – usually economic. These extensions, however, do not necessarily augment, and the merely recent is rarely in any larger sense beneficial.

One remembers the Zen precept that whatever you do should be done wholly and single-mindedly. When you eat, you eat; when you sleep, you sleep; when you meditate, you meditate. Through this, singleness and depth are reached.

This, always more of an ambition than an accomplishment, is now even further removed. When you eat and drive while attending to your Walkman or portable TV or trying to see who has just called you on your phone, you do none of these things wholly and single-mindedly.

Precisely, all attempts at defining self are stilled. And you are left with only the proliferating image.

Sources

Asahi Shinbun, 23 February 1997

Ashby, Janet, 'When in Doubt Just Say: Wakarimasen', *The Japanese Times*,
    12 May 2002

Asano Kensuke, *Mainichi Shinbun*, 17 January 1999

Austin, Mark, 'Constructing a Japanese Identity', *Daily Yomiuri*,
    11 November 2001

Barthes, Roland, *Mythologies* (Paris, 1957, trans. Annette Lavers, London, 2000)

—, *Empire of Signs* (Paris, 1972, trans. Richard Howard, New York, 1982)

—, *The Eiffel Tower and other Mythologies*, trans. Richard Howard
    (Berkeley, 1979)

Bates, Clive, 'Teens May Drop Smokes for Cellphones', *Japan Times*,
    4 November 2000

Befu Harumi, *Hegemony of Homogeneity* (Melbourne, 2001)

Brasor, Philip, 'Uniqlo: Seeing the Brand of No Brand as Brand', *Japan Times*,
    4 May 2000

—, 'Meet your Future Friend, Mr Roboto', *Japan Times*, 18 January 2001

Braun, Stuart, 'Fashion Frenzy', *Metropolis*, 26 April 2000

Cassirer, Ernst, *An Essay on Man* (New Haven, 1944), p. 43 [cited by Neil Postman]

Chalfen, Richard, and Mai Murui, 'Print Club Photography in Japan: Framing
    Social Relationships', *Visual Sociology*, 16 (2001)

Clark, Gregory, 'The Japanese People *Are* Different', *Japan Times*, 8 October 2000

Cullen, Lisa Takeuchi, 'Rent Boys', *TIME*, 21 January 2002

Culler, Jonathan, *Barthes* (Oxford, 1983)

Daimon Sayuri, *Japan Times*, 19 August 2001

Drake, Kate, *TIME*, 25 June 2001

Feldman, Edmund, *Art as Image and Idea* (New Jersey, 1967)

Fitzpatrick, Michael, *Daily Telegraph* [London], 13 April 2000 [citing comments by
    Hachiya Kazuhiko and Nakamura Yasuko]

French, Howard, 'Kabukicho's Siren Song Lures Young Women', *International
    Herald-Tribune*, 16 November 2001

Fuller, Thomas, *International Herald Tribune*, 26–7 May 2001

Gibson, William, 'Modern Boys and Mobile Girls', *Japan Times*, 7 April 2001

Hoffman, Michael, 'You Gotta Have Wa, or Do You?', *Japan Times*,
    17 February 2002

Hollingworth, Will, *Japan Times*, 2 March 2001

Horvat, Andrew, *Japanese Beyond Words* (Berkeley, 2000)

'I-mode's Virtual Love Games Strike a Chord', *Daily Yomiuri*, 22 December 2000

Inwood, Shane, 'Pachi Puro: the New Math of the New Pachinko Professional',
    JapanZine (November 2001)

Ishige Naomichi, cited in Linhard & Frühstück, *The Culture of Japan as Seen through
    its Leisure* (Albany, 1998)

Ito Masami, 'New Ways to Kei-mmunication', *Japan Times*, 1 December 2002

Iyer, Pico, 'Finding the Old in the New', *TIME*, 1 May 2000

Joseph, Sam, 'A.I.', *Japan, Inc.* (November 2001)

Kawabata Kenji, *Mainichi Shinbun*, 1 January 2001

Kawanishi Yuko, 'Call Me if You Can't Connect', *Asahi Shinbun*, 22 March, 2002

Keane, Marc, *Kyoto Journal*, 41 (1999)

Keene, Donald, *Landscapes and Portraits* (Tokyo, 1971)

Kehr, Dave, 'A Second Golden Age Arrives for Japanese Film', *International Herald-
    Tribune*, 22 January 2002

Kenko Yoshida, *Tsurigusa* (Essays in idleness) [1330]; cited in Keene

Koch, Jacinta, 'Go, Ganguro', *Courier-Mail* [Brisbane], 3 March 2000

Large, Tim, *Daily Yomiuri*, 10 September 1999

Linhard, Sepp, and Sabine Frühstück, *The Culture of Japan as Seen through its
    Leisure* (Albany, 1998)

MacNeil, Robert, 'Is Television Shortening our Attention Span?', *New York
    University Education Quarterly* (Winter 1983) [cited by Neil Postman]

McClure, Steve, 'Cell Phones ringing to Latest Pop Tunes', *Mainichi Daily News*,
    8 January 2001

McQuillin, Kristen, 'Robotops', *Metropolis*, 22 March 2002

McVeigh, Brian, *Wearing Ideology* (Oxford, 2000)

Manzenreiter, Wolfram, 'Time, Space & Money: Cultural Dimensions of the Pachinko Game', in Linhard and Frühstück, *The Culture of Japan as Seen through its Leisure* (Albany, 1998)

Markus, Andrew L., 'The Carnivals of Edo', *Harvard Journal of Asiatic Studies*, XLV/2 (December 1985)

Martin, Judith, 'Miss Manners', *Japan Times*, 28 January 2001

Mead, Rebecca, 'Shopping Rebellion', *New Yorker*, 18 March 2002

Miyao Shigeo, 'Manga', *Kodansha Encyclopedia of Japan*

Mori Akiko, *Japan Times*, 14 November 2001

Morikawa, Kathleen, 'Vigilante's Calling', *Asahi Shinbun*, 20 March 2001

Murakami Mitsuko, *Asiaweek*, 3 February 2000

Naito Minoru, *Nikkei Weekly*, 27 December 1999

Nakamura Mariko, 'Girls Laugh off Danger Signals', *Asahi Evening News*, 4 July 2000

Nakamura Usagi, 'Vernacular Views', *Japan Times*, 15 March 2002

Natsume Fusanosuke, 'Japan's Manga Culture', *Japan Foundation Newsletter*, XXVII/3–4 (March 2000)

Nishiyama Matsunosuke, *Edo Culture: Daily Life and Diversions in Urban Japan, 1600–1868* (Honolulu, 1997)

Palmer, Kimberly, 'Match Play', *Asahi Shinbun*, 16–17 February 2002

Paskal, Cleo, 'Travel ...', *New York Times*, 5 June 1995

Plotz, David, 'Pachinko', *Slate*, 19 April 2002

Postman, Neil, *Amusing Ourselves to Death: Public Discourse in the Age of Show Business* (New York, 1985)

Pountain, Dick, and David Robins, *Cool Rules: Anatomy of an Attitude* (London, 2000)

Prideaux, Eric, *Mainichi Daily News*, 21 June 2000

—, *Japan Times*, 2 April 2002

Richie, Donald, 'The Tongue of Fashion', 'Pachinko', *A Lateral View* (Berkeley, 1992)

—, 'The Sex Market', 'Patterns of Leisure', *Partial Views* (Tokyo, 1995)

Sato Kenji, 'More Animated than Life', *Kyoto Journal*, 41 (1999)

Sato Noriko, 'Many Seeking Comfort in "Character Goods" as Security Blankets, Survey Shows', *Daily Yomiuri*, 10 April 2001

Sawa Keiichiro, *Mainichi Shinbun*, 22 October 2000

Sawa Takamitsu, *Japan Times*, 2 May 1991

Schodt, Frederick L., *Manga! Manga! The World of Japanese Comics* (Tokyo, 1983)

—, *Dreamland Japan: Writings on Modern Manga* (Berkeley, 1996)

Schreiber, Mark, 'Freed from Cells: Japanese Ditching Their Mobiles',
 Japan Times, 6 October 2002

Seidensticker, Edward, *Low City, High City* (New York, 1983)

Shinomiya Yasuo 'Cell-phone Dating Boom Brings New Dangers',
 Yomiuri Shinbun, 21 June 2001

Shoji Kaori, 'Searching for the Japanese Cool', *Japan Times*, 10 September 1999

—, 'Let's Hear It for the Big Wa in a Small Country', *Japan Times*,
 18 October 2002

Soeda Yoshiya, 'Comic Magazines', *Kodansha Encyclopedia of Japan*

Suwa Keichiro, *Mainichi Daily News*, 22 October 2000

Tada Michitaro, *Asobu to Nihonjin* (Tokyo, 1984) [cited by Manzenreiter]

Terashima Shin'ichi, 'Japan Could Use More Logic, Less Poetry', *Japan Times*, 23
 October 1999

Thompson, Mark, 'More to Life than This', *Japan Times*, 28 May 1997

Tosa Mitsuoki, *Honcho Gaho Taiden* (Authoritative summary of the rules of
 Japanese painting) [*c.* 1678]; cited in Ueda Makoto, *Literary and Art Theories in
 Japan* (Honolulu, 1967)

Trifonas, Peter, *Barthes and 'The Empire of Signs'* (London, 2001)

Urenaka Taiga, 'Are Cell Phones Becoming too Disruptive?', *Japan Times*,
 8 February 2002

Veblen, Thorstein, *A Theory of the Leisure Class* (New York, 1899)

Watts, Jonathan, *The Guardian*, 2 May 2000

Willis, Bruce, reported in *Mainichi Daily News*, 18 May 1997

Yakushiji Sayaka, 'Toy Boys', *Asahi Shimbun*, 14 April 2002

Zitowitz, Philip, 'Uniformly Stylish Japanese', *Japan Times*, 19 August 2001

THE LIBRARY
SAINT FRANCIS XAVIER
SIXTH FORM COLLEGE
MALWOOD ROAD, SW12 8EN